D1186842

THE TYPO GRAPHIC UNIVERSE

THE TYPOGRAPHIC UNIV

STEVEN HELLER & GAIL ANDERSON

OGRA RA

LETTERFORMS FOUND IN NATURE,
THE BUILT WORLD AND HUMAN IMAGINATION

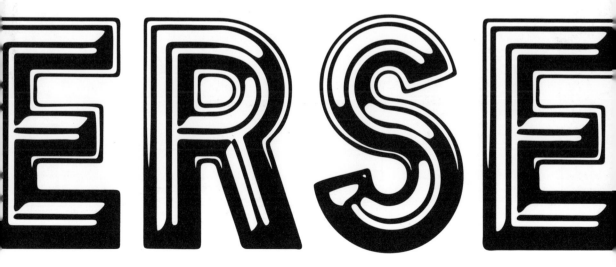

ERSE

Thames & Hudson

For Seymour Chwast –S.H.

For Paula Scher –G.A.

STEVEN HELLER is co-chair of the MFA Design "Designer as Author + Entrepreneur" program at New York's School of Visual Arts. He is the author, co-author, or editor of more than 165 books on graphic design, typography, and popular culture. Heller is in the Art Directors Hall of Fame, and was the recipient of the AIGA Lifetime Achievement Medal in 1999, and the Smithsonian Institution National Design Award for "Design Mind" in 2011.

GAIL ANDERSON is a New York-based designer, educator, and partner at Anderson Newton Design who also teaches at the School of Visual Arts. In 2008, she received the Lifetime Achievement Medal from the AIGA. Anderson also serves on the Citizens' Stamp Advisory Committee for the United States Post Office.

ACKNOWLEDGMENTS

The universe is full of typography, as the title of this book suggests, and we hope that we've managed to capture some of the best of it. We are indebted to our many contributors for their enthusiasm and cooperation, as well as to our intrepid researchers, Abigail Steinem and young Betsy Mei Chun Lin. Without Abby and Betsy, our *Universe* would be a whole lot smaller and much less interesting.

Our gratitude is extended to Lucas Dietrich and Theresa Morgan at Thames & Hudson for their patience and encouragement throughout the production of this book. Without them, our *Universe* would be nonexistent.

Finally, we'd like to thank David Rhodes, President, and Anthony Rhodes, Executive Vice President, of the School of Visual Arts; as well as Lita Talarico, co-chair of the MFA Design "Designer as Author + Entrepreneur" program. And to Louise Fili and Nicolas Heller, thanks for everything good.

Cover letters include typography from Mervyn Burlanksy, Andrew Byrom, Studio Kalle Mattsson, Dutch Osborne, Erik Varusio, and Thijs Verbeek. Image opposite by Christian Brandt (see page 200).

RESEARCH
Abigail Steinem
Betsy Mei Chun Lin

First published in the United Kingdom in 2014 by Thames & Hudson Ltd, 181A High Holborn, London WC1V 7QX

The Typographic Universe © 2014 Steven Heller and Gail Anderson

Designed by Anderson Newton Design

British Library Cataloguing-in-Publication Data
A catalogue record for this book is available from the British Library

ISBN 978-0-500-24145-5

Printed and bound in China by Toppan Leefung Printing Limited

To find out about all our publications, please visit **www.thamesandhudson.com**. There you can subscribe to our e-newsletter, browse or download our current catalogue, and buy any titles that are in print.

FOUND TYPE IS NEVER LOST

OH SMEXY "M" The "smexy legs" of Minkyeong Lee's dog, Coco, create just the right alphabetic mood. PHOTOGRAPHER: Minkyeong Lee LOCATION: Queens, NY

HERE IS A CURIOUSLY THERAPEUTIC PSYCHOLOGICAL condition called pareidolia that allows humans to perceive faces in places where they do not actually exist. These special venues are often patterned, such as clouds, shag bathmats, or marble tabletops. If you look at them a certain way, *voilà*! A face instantly materializes, but blink or refocus your eye a millimeter to one side or the other and the illusion disappears forever. Well, this imaginary face does not have be solely human or animal. It can also be a *type*face, or any other alphabetic symbol. If you cast your eye up to the sky or down to the ground, there's an excellent likelihood you'll discover something that either looks like a letter or actually is one. That's the focus of this book: we've collected together images of unexpected letterforms found in natural, artificial, and urban environments, as well as examples of the unusual, original, and often eccentric types created by designers both accidentally and deliberately.

In our previous three books together, *New Vintage Type, New Ornamental Type*, and *New Modernist Type*, we surveyed a range of quirky and eclectic type styles, both handmade and digitally rendered. We looked at the way that old and passé letterforms have been revived, renewed, and rehabilitated for contemporary use with little flairs and flicks. The results have been reinvigorating for typographers and graphic designers, and have brightened up the printed page. *The Typographic Universe* is the logical next step in our typo-madness.

Typography styled out of non-traditional sources is not a new phenomenon. Alphabetic topiary – trees and bushes clipped into the shapes of letters and words – has long been a feature of landscape gardening, for instance. Metaphorical faces made out of anything, from animate to inanimate objects, have also been around for a while, an offshoot, perhaps, of the typographic *trompe l'œil*. The Italian Renaissance painter Giuseppe Arcimboldo,

famed for his *Vertumnus* and other composite portrait heads, is a possible precursor to some of the floral letterforms included here.

The current popularity of serendipitous lettering has both professional and amateur designers combing the globe (and Google Earth) with digital cameras and Photoshop apps in search of truly surprising letters: from the uncanny shapes formed by negative spaces between city skyscrapers to contorted alphabets of torn underwear. With a fusion of strong craft, determination, and a quick imagination, virtually anything can be used to make letters. Once you've seen the extensive examples of typographic conjuring assembled here, you won't need to concentrate hard to visualize invisible faces. You'll spot typefaces galore, just like we do, wherever we roam.

– SH & GA

WATERY Look hard enough, long enough, or wishfully enough, and a letter will appear almost anywhere. Here, the setting sun makes a lowercase "i." PHOTOGRAPHER: Minkyeong Lee LOCATION: Venice, Italy

ALPHABETS OF
EVERYDAY THINGS

RULER "N" Photography/design duo Francois and Jane Robert find the unusual in the usual, the everyday, and the commonplace. Letterforms appear to them like secret glyphs ringing from the unconscious to the conscious. PHOTOGRAPHER: Francois Robert/Francois Robert Photography LOCATION: Tucson, AZ © Francois Robert

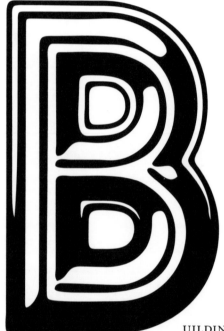

UILDING LETTERS OUT OF OBJECTS IS AN AMBITIOUS KIND of visual punning. Even if one has the eye and hand to create the most imaginative connections, the outcome is still questionable. An alphabet made from non-typographic materials can either be a brilliant concept or bad pun. The latter – letters that stretch the "joke" beyond being funny – must be avoided. The examples here fulfill their promise and come off smart.

VENETIAN This stencil typeface was commissioned by *Elle Decoration*. Fittingly for a magazine about interior design, the letters were inspired by the forms created by opening and closing Venetian blinds. DESIGNER: The Office of Andrew Byrom CLIENT: *Elle Decoration* (UK) LOCATION: London

HARDER, BETTER, FASTER, STRONGER Students at the University of Washington were asked to use a line from a song to develop original display letterforms. "The letterforms should be inspired by the lyrics, artists, or anything relevant to the song. Consider musical history, instruments, and symbolism. Use any materials or processes you like, as long as the letters do not originate from the computer," instructed the brief. DESIGNER: Van Hoang LOCATION: Seattle, WA

BLOODCLOT The letters in this typeface, originally designed for a Type Directors Club promotional flyer, are based on the shapes of various Band Aids. The experiment led to the creation of a full-character digital typeface called "Bloodclot." DESIGNER: The Office of Andrew Byrom CLIENT: Type Directors Club LOCATION: London

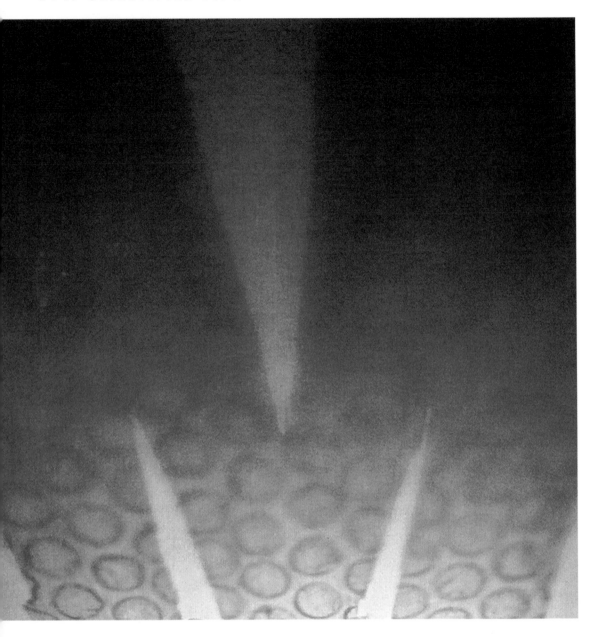

EXPERIMENTAL TYPE Billie May used found materials to construct a range of letterforms based on Futura Extra Bold Condensed. This particular example was made with bubble wrap. "I wanted my fabrications to resemble the characteristics of Futura," the designer explained, "while creating another dimension of texture, light, and shade. I created only a few letters of the alphabet in order to work quickly and establish successful results that clearly demonstrate examples of my experimental typeface. To contrast with the geometric, sans serif Futura I also experimented with Garamond, a more traditional light serif. However, I found that most of my chosen media were more effective when using Futura Medium and Extra Bold Condensed as templates."
DESIGNER: Billie May LOCATION: Brighton, UK

TRUMPET TYPOGRAPHY Graham Hauser created this "C" with "one trumpet, one band saw, and one camera on one sunny day in Indiana."
DESIGNER: Graham Hauser LOCATION: Upland, IN

TILE TYPE To make this typeface, Michelle Pappas cracked ceramic test tiles with a screwdriver. "By using a screwdriver, I could not control the way the tiles broke," she said. "I then arranged the broken pieces to create letters out of the negative space." DESIGNER: Michelle Pappas LOCATION: Chicago, IL

MUGGING LETTERS What you see may not always be what you've got. When viewed from above, this travel coffee mug takes on another form, transforming into the letter "Q." PHOTOGRAPHER: Megan Daley LOCATION: New York, NY

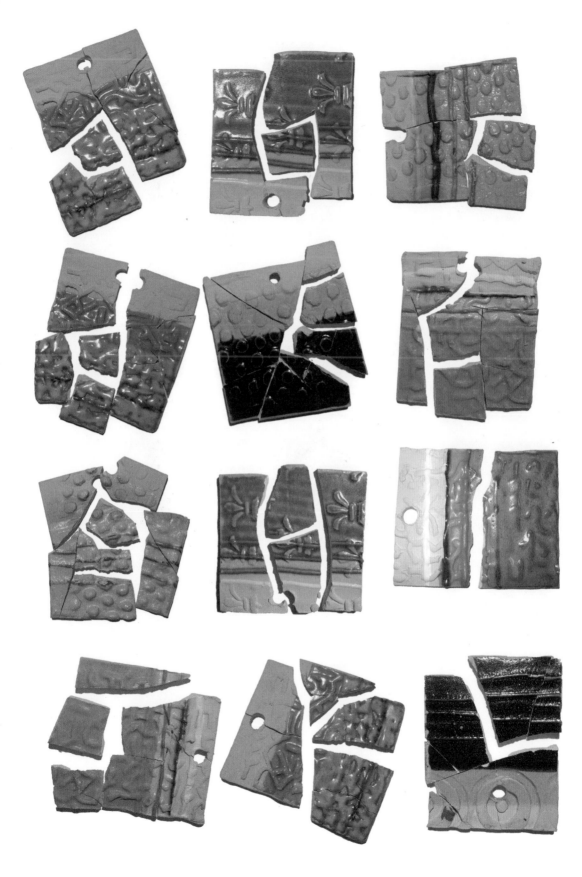

BROOKLYN SAFARI In 2013, students from Gail Anderson's "Just Type" class, part of the MFA Design program at New York's School of Visual Arts, were asked to trek through the labyrinthine streets of Brooklyn on a hunt for hidden letters.
PHOTOGRAPHER: Sasha Prood LOCATION: Brooklyn, NY

ALPHABET CHAIRS For this assignment, Sarah Croughwell and her classmates were given one hour to find or create an alphabet using objects typically found on campus.
PHOTOGRAPHER: Sarah Croughwell LOCATION: Lowell, MA

ABC BOOKCASE The idea for this shelving came to Eva Alessandrini and Roberto Saporiti while they were designing letters within a basic square shape. "We imagined the construction line of the letters as shelves within three-dimensional square units, and the direct result was the physical realization of a piece of furniture," they explained. "'Read Your Bookcase' seemed the most appropriate sentence, an exhortation to read, both the content and the container!" DESIGNERS: Eva Alessandrini, Roberto Saporiti LOCATION: Besnate, Italy

SHOESTRING ALPHABET As part of the undergraduate Design program at the University of Texas at Arlington, Pamela Speck and her fellow students were asked to work with their hands, rather than computer pixels, to construct an alphabet out of materials not normally used for crafting letters. DESIGNER: Pamela Speck/Violet Fox Visuals LOCATION: Arlington, TX

THE ONE SHOW ANNUAL "The theme was a celebration of New York City's tireless spirit," said Graham Clifford of this cover design. "We called in Peter Cunningham, who roamed the city on his bicycle, photographing signs and storefronts to make the words and titles we needed." DESIGNER: Graham Clifford Design PHOTOGRAPHER: Peter Cunningham ART DIRECTOR: Graham Clifford CLIENT: The One Club LOCATION: New York, NY

ZIPPER "V" Spotted on the L subway line, this hoodie is alternately an "M" and a "V." PHOTOGRAPHER: Muddyum LOCATION: Brooklyn, NY

MY TYPE OF FILM This metaphorical typeface was
created by arranging the tape from an old video cassette into
letterforms, a way of reusing an item that had become obsolete.
DESIGNER: Ceol Ryder LOCATION: Limerick, Ireland

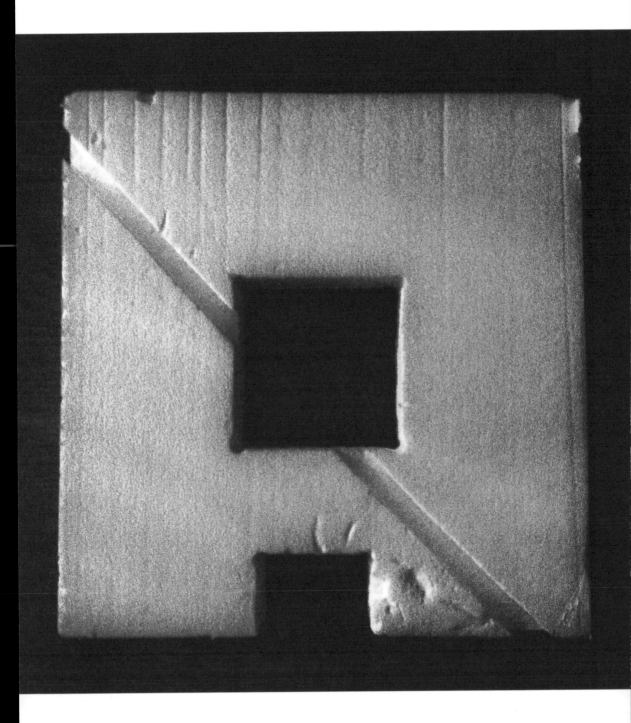

ABCDEVERYWHERE Zipeng Zhu began with a simple premise: letterforms can be found everywhere and anywhere. He set out to prove that his theory was true.
PHOTOGRAPHER: Zipeng Zhu LOCATION: New York, NY

WICKER "S" Francois and Jane Robert traverse the globe
searching for the typographic manifestations in man-made
and natural objects that most non-designers cannot see.
PHOTOGRAPHER: Jane Robert/Francois Robert Photography
LOCATION: Bergun, Switzerland © Francois Robert

2   L   0   O   1   V   3   E!

LOVE 2013! Robert Appleton recognized the word "LOVE" in a selection of objects scattered randomly on his mother's bathroom shelf in Kirkintilloch, Scotland. He rearranged the "letters" and photographed them, later adding the date and exclamation mark. The design was then distributed digitally via email and Facebook. DESIGNER: Robert Appleton LOCATION: Toronto

TREBLE CLEF This treble clef, hand-crafted from fabric and suspended in space, was made for an article in *Economia* magazine. DESIGNER: Charles Williams PHOTOGRAPHER: Jim Campbell ART DIRECTOR: Sarah Barnett CLIENT: *Economia* LOCATION: London

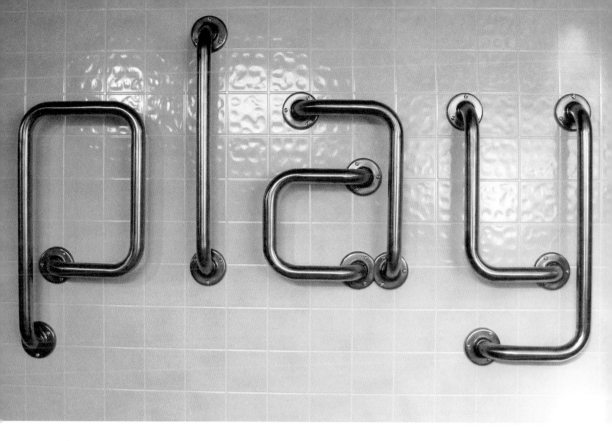

GRAB-ME These letters were constructed "using the same materials and principles of bathroom handrails (or grab-bars). The design adheres almost perfectly to the idea of typographic stencils." DESIGNER: The Office of Andrew Byrom CLIENT: *The New York Times Magazine* LOCATION: Long Beach, CA

SHADOW TYPE In 2010, Burcu Celiksap created a shadow alphabet using small metal and white plastic everyday objects such as nail scissors or hair pins. "The aim of the project is to gain consciousness of the environment," she said. "To represent everyday experience while arranging typefaces and documenting them with photography." DESIGNER: Burcu Celiksap LOCATION: Izmir, Turkey

FURNITURE ALPHABET The typography used in this campaign for a home furnishings store successfully showcased a range of furniture designs. "Execution was a beast," recalled The Butler Bros. "Every shot is an actual piece of furniture from the inventory of High Fashion Home. Every shot is practical. This was a no Photoshop affair."
DESIGNER: The Butler Bros PHOTOGRAPHER: Adam Voorhes
CLIENT: High Fashion Home LOCATION: Austin, TX

REALITY Jacqueline Wong created alternative letterforms out of lipsticks, mascaras, powders, and other beauty aids to "address how makeup alters our perception of what is real and what isn't." DESIGNER: Jacqueline Wong LOCATION: Toronto

WOOD TYPE "This is a font with a strong sculptural quality of wood," explained Txaber Mentxaka. Each letter is constructed from irregular planes with different orientations, which gives the structure the dimensionality of a finished piece of furniture. DESIGNER: Txaber Mentxaka LOCATION: Bilbao

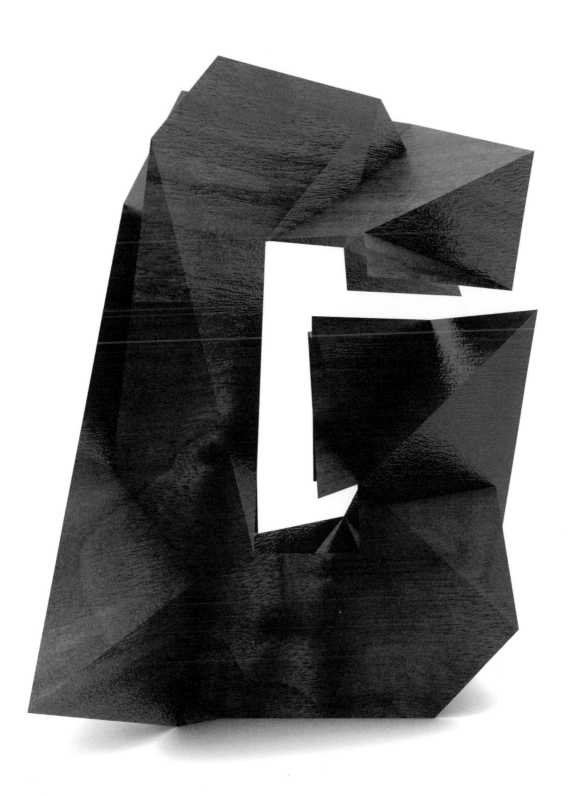

PAPER MODULES Txaber Mentxaka built an entire alphabet out of hundreds of paper circles. The resulting letterforms are suggestive of ever-expanding, fungal-like organisms. DESIGNER: Txaber Mentxaka LOCATION: Bilbao

CONDOM TYPE This type is made out of, well, condoms. "It's a part of my ever-growing experimental handmade typography project called 'Diary Type,'" Vladimir Končar explained. "'Diary Type' is a kind of personal typographic diary that started as a experiment in 2007. I collect various objects and from them I form letters. With those letters I write down my thoughts, and they become a symbolic link between the font and my reflections." (See also pages 42, 101, 112, 128, 280, and 298.) DESIGNER: Vladimir Končar LOCATION: Zagreb

CLOTH TYPE From a distance, these words seem to be made from an oozing substance. They were created by draping a typographic framework in white cloth to give the illusion of a slow flow. DESIGNER: Txaber Mentxaka LOCATION: Bilbao

"S" RUBBER BAND "This is an object I found walking the streets of Brooklyn," said Muddyum. PHOTOGRAPHER: Muddyum LOCATION: Brooklyn, NY

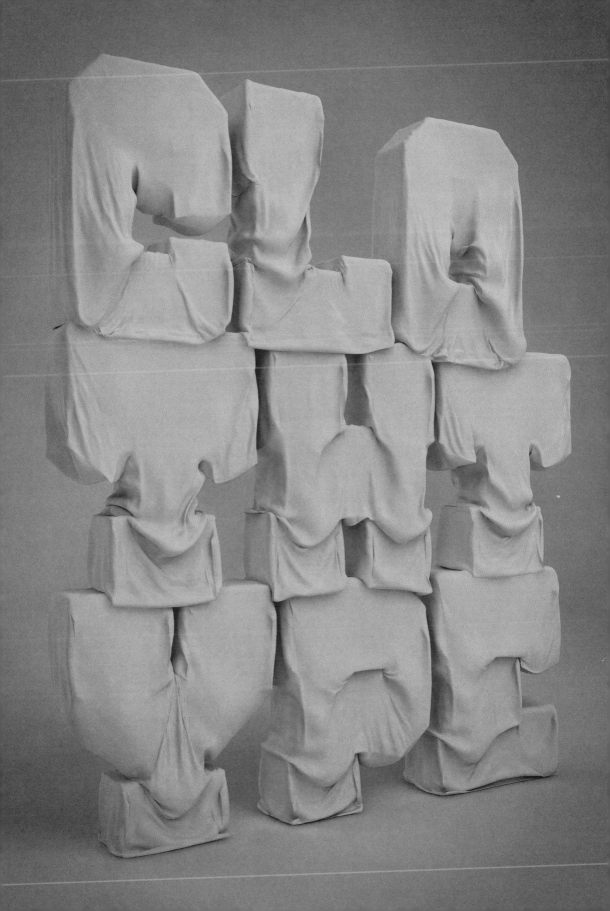

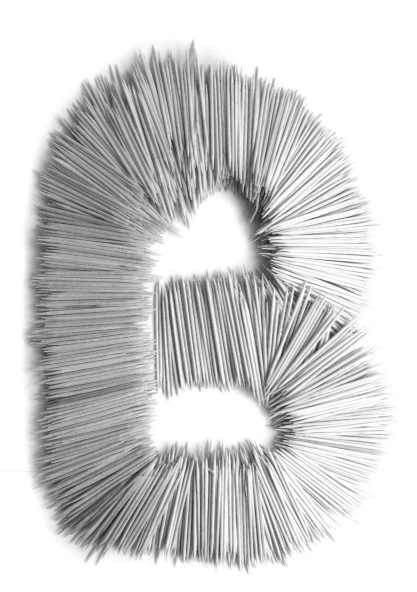

ADORMECIDA
A promotional poster
for *Adormecida* (Asleep),
a puppet play in which
the two main characters
leave the city in search of
a new world. They travel
to a rural place, where
they become trapped by
wool strings, symbolizing
their inability to escape
their vicious urban
habits. "I developed a
handmade poster, where
the letters are made
with 350m of wool,"
Sérgio Alves explained.
"I organized the letters
to look like a branch of
a tree – the 'tree of life.'"
DESIGNER: Sérgio Alves/
Atelier d'alves CLIENT:
Teatro e Marionetas de
Mandrágora LOCATION:
Porto, Portugal

TOOTHPICK TYPE An experimental typeface constructed out of toothpicks from
Vladimir Končar's "Diary Type" project (see pages 38, 101, 112, 128, 280, and 298).
DESIGNER: Vladimir Končar LOCATION: Zagreb

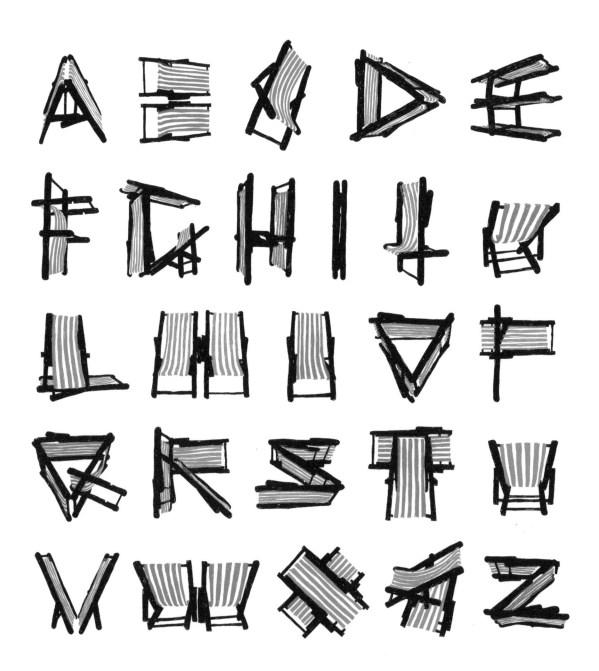

DECKCHAIR ALPHABET Sarah Hyndman placed scale models of deckchairs in different arrangements to create the letters of the alphabet. "Each letter is hand drawn and the final collection screen-printed as a poster," she explained.
DESIGNER: Sarah Hyndman LOCATION: London

SÁBADO 28 DE JULIO / 21 HRS.
Tabasco 324 int. 201 (entre Oaxaca y Valladolid)

DESPEDIDA For this animated party invitation,
Abril Salas formed the word *"despedida"* (farewell) from
colored lights set against a vintage wallpaper background.
DESIGNER: Abril Salas LOCATION: Mexico City

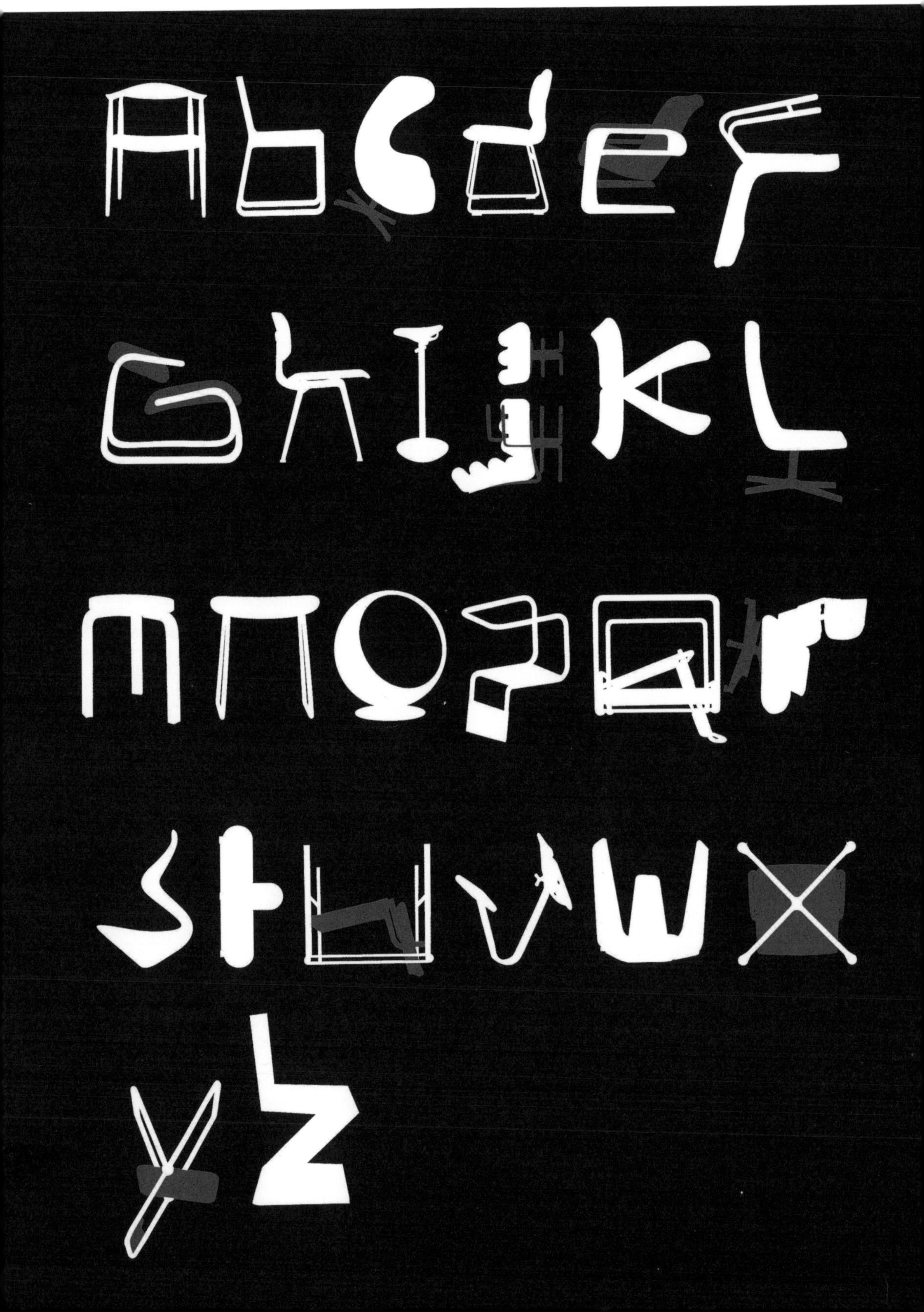

TYPESEAT Tim Fishlock's pictorial alphabet is "made up of some of the most iconic chairs of the 20th century." DESIGNER: Tim Fishlock LOCATION: London

BIKE TO LIFE "The goal was to create an alphabet, build words, and compose posters with images of bike corpses," explained Toormix. In this way, the dilapidated cycles are brought back to life. DESIGNERS: Oriol Armengou, Ferran Mitjans, Gerard Marin/Toormix LOCATION: Barcelona

EL MÓN DELS NENS (THE WORLD OF CHILDREN) This lettering was
created for a fictitious kids' newspaper supplement. The key objective was
"to make an alphabet that was interesting for both parents and children."
DESIGNER: Mòn Castel LOCATION: Barcelona

ABCHAIRS An alphabet to sit on and a series of 26 chairs and stools to form words with. These prototypes were made from lacquered MDF, with the final limited-edition pieces manufactured upon request. DESIGNER: Roeland Otten PHOTOGRAPHER: Bas Helbers LOCATION: Rotterdam

CHANNELED LIGHT Troy Hyde was inspired to create this font "by those shapes found at the cross-section of a cylindrical roll of paper, rolled in different ways." He chose corrugated paper "because of its thicker edge, which can be made to form a decorative detail." DESIGNER: Troy Hyde LOCATION: London

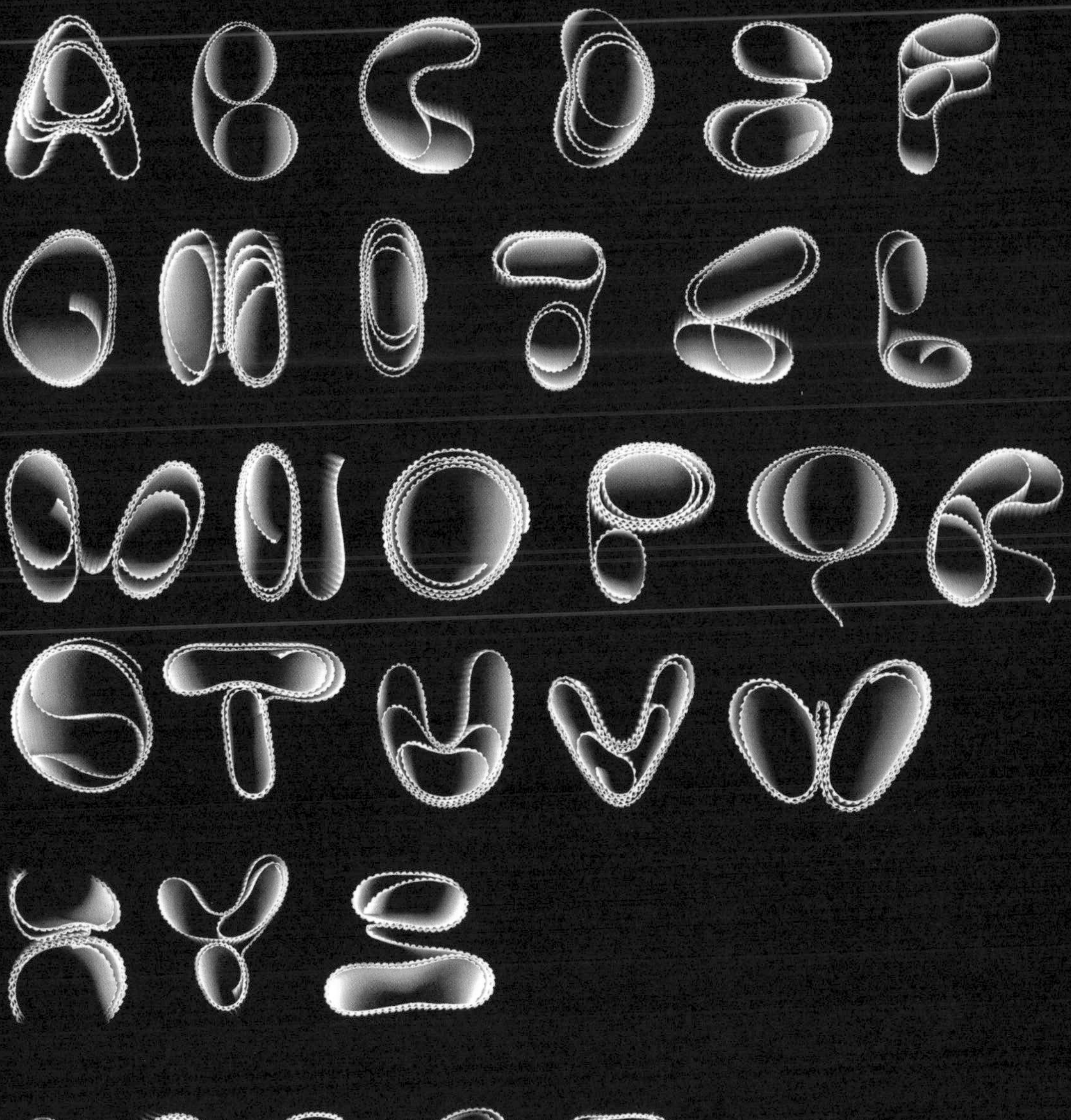
ABCDEF
GHIJKL
MNOPQR
STUVW
XYZ
12345
67890

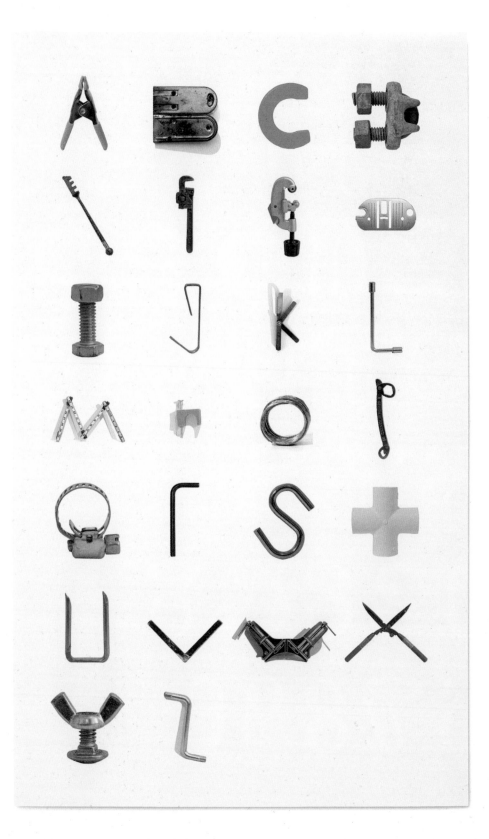

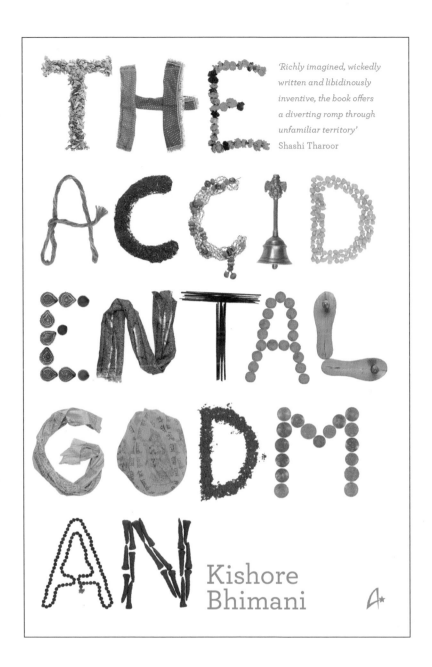

THE
ACCID
ENTAL
GODM
AN

'Richly imagined, wickedly
written and libidinously
inventive, the book offers
a diverting romp through
unfamiliar territory'
Shashi Tharoor

Kishore
Bhimani

TYPOGRAPHIC TOOLS Jenna Robert
collected both old and new precision tools that
resembled letters, photographed each one, and
then displayed the images together to create
an entire alphabet. DESIGNER: Jenna Robert
LOCATION: Provo, UT

THE ACCIDENTAL GODMAN Kishore Bhimani's
novel tells the story of the transformation of the
"ungodly" prince Ranvijay into a Godman, a
charismatic guru claiming spiritual attainment.
The design concept for the cover was "based on
the ingredients needed 'to become' a Godman,"
reported Ishan Khosla. DESIGNER: Ishan Khosla
ILLUSTRATORS: Vineet Kaur, Mayank Thakur
PHOTOGRAPHER: Mayank Thakur CLIENT:
Amaryllis Publishing LOCATION: New Delhi

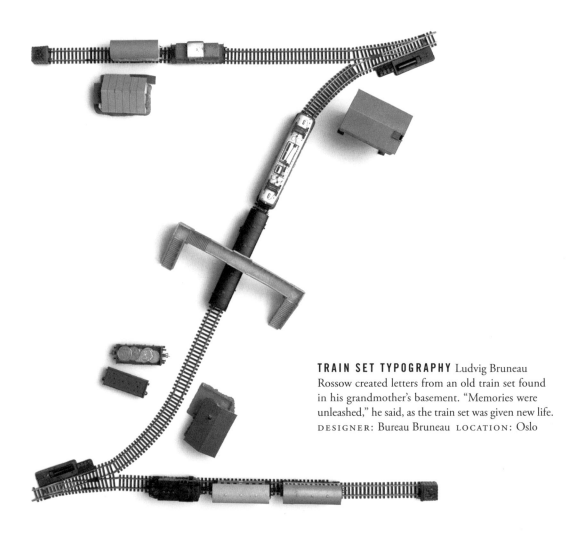

TRAIN SET TYPOGRAPHY Ludvig Bruneau
Rossow created letters from an old train set found
in his grandmother's basement. "Memories were
unleashed," he said, as the train set was given new life.
DESIGNER: Bureau Bruneau LOCATION: Oslo

PHOTOGRAM ALPHABET The making of this typeface involved the camera-less photographic process
known as the photogram, in which a negative shadow image is captured on light-sensitive paper. There
is no distortion of scale between the images and the found, recycled, and reused objects from which
they are cast. "As each object has a unique shape, the signature of the shadow is always a surprise,"
noted Dutch Osborne. "As a collection, these signatures have begun to define a new typography and
an attitude towards reuse and appropriation. While some images are familiar to adults, others present
themselves to children. The purpose of the piece is to foster a dialog of discovery and exchange."
DESIGNER: Dutch Osborne LOCATION: Brooklyn, NY

PAPER TYPE Txaber Mentxaka used different combinations of paper modules to build a three-dimensional alphabet. He then set the sculptural letterforms on fire. DESIGNER: Txaber Mentxaka LOCATION: Bilbao

WARUM IST DAS SO? (WHY IS THAT?) Letterforms from one of the chapter dividers in *Erforsche Deine Welt* (Explore Your World), a children's science book that aims to inspire its young readers to become scientists and learn the secrets of nature. Lisa Rienermann created this lavish typography out of the materials used in the experiments detailed in the subsequent pages. DESIGNER: Lisa Rienermann CLIENT: Beltz & Gelberg LOCATION: Berlin

IST DAS SO?

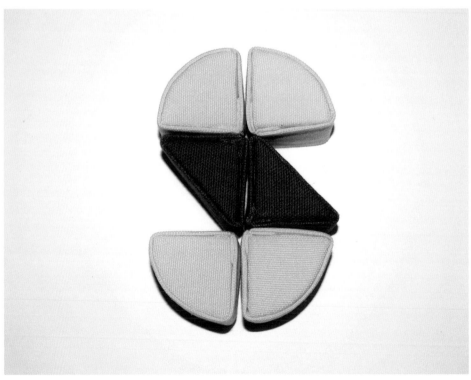

FABRIC TYPE Chua Wenjing used a set of geometric fabric blocks to create infinite possibilities of type in a process that challenged design conventions. "Through the method of random construction and deconstruction, the fabric prototype seeks to extend the ways designers perceive typography by creating sensually perceptible fabric blocks that would aid them in the generation of creative typographic outcomes," she explained. DESIGNER: Chua Wenjing LOCATION: Singapore

TOKYO, PARIS, NEW YORK This advertising concept for a travel agency took photographs of famous sites, foods, and brand logos, as well as other iconic images associated with a particular city, and turned them into letterforms that spelled out the name of the place. As the designer explained: "Each object in the typography meaningfully conveys the message and strengthens the promotion." DESIGNER: Raina Lee CLIENT: STA Travel LOCATION: Australia

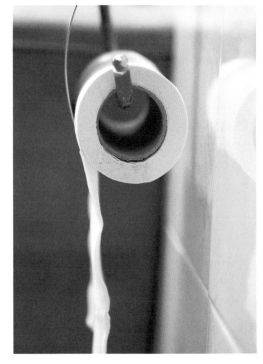

BATHROOM ALPHABET Yap Ning was commissioned to find and photograph letterforms in his everyday life. "I decided to limit myself to one place…and chose the bathroom, an often overlooked yet essential part of our lives," he said. "It was surprising how common household objects could form a letter when looked at from a different perspective. I also left my bathroom as it was – hair, stains, and all – to reflect how very mundane and 'everyday' the setting was."
PHOTOGRAPHER: Yap Ning
LOCATION: Singapore

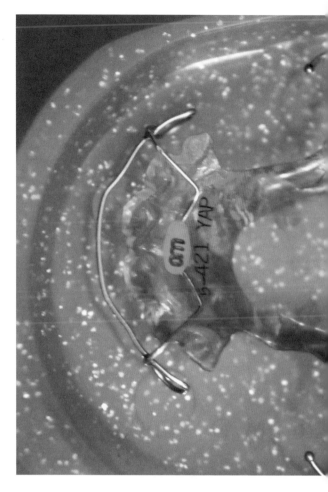

TABLE FOR TWO "In homage to the fabulous curves and dynamic line weights of the great American type designer Herb Lubalin (and his unsung genius letterer Tom Carnase), the Table for Two is modeled on one of his [Lubalin's] voluptuous 1970s ampersands for *U&lc* magazine," explained Matt Innes. "Construction was inspired by the simplicity of surfboard fins – the legs are attached with a precision-fit slot-and-tab technique." There are no nails or screws, just hardwood ply cut with a CNC router, glued by hand, and finished with Scandinavian oil and beeswax. DESIGNERS: Matt Innes, Saori Kajiwara/Device Independent PHOTOGRAPHER: Aaron Walker LOCATION: Melbourne

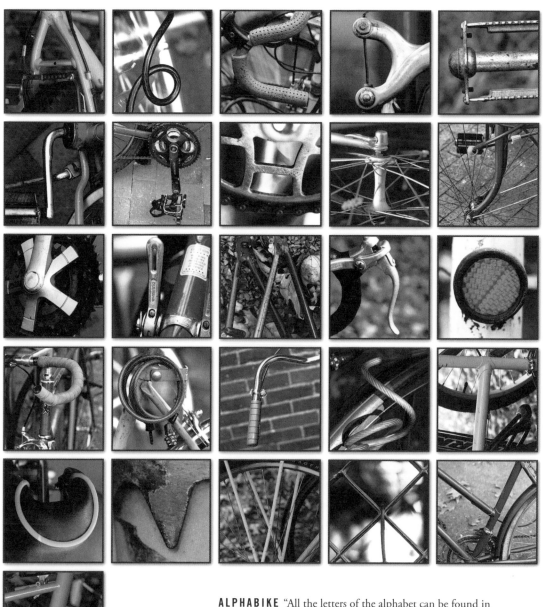

ALPHABIKE "All the letters of the alphabet can be found in your bike if you know where to look," explained Molly McLeod. "The 'Alphabike' poster was a self-initiated project created out of a desire to find letterforms in my favorite mode of transportation." DESIGNER: Molly McLeod LOCATION: Amherst, MA

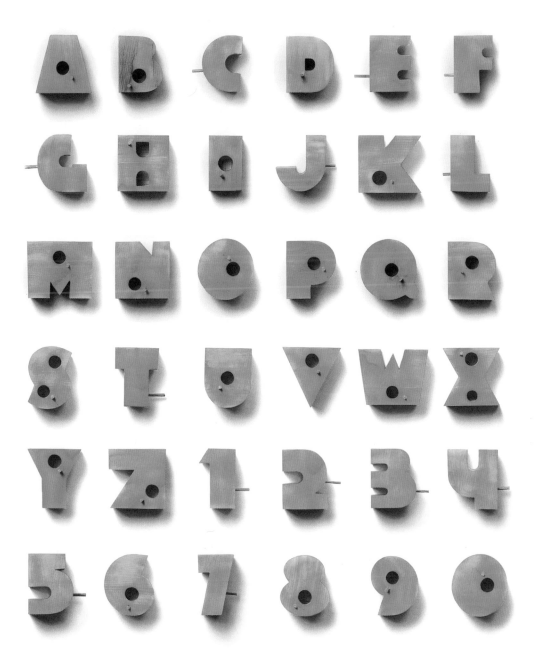

LIVING TYPOGRAPHY Nishant Jethi carved an entire alphabet and the numbers 0 to 9 out of wood. The hollow, three-dimensional forms also function as bird's nest boxes, which he sent to friends and family to use as house numbers or nameplates. "House sparrows were once everywhere," he observed. "It seemed that they were untouchable, but now there is a sharp decline in their number because of the lack of nesting and breeding spaces. With high rises and malls coming up everywhere, the birds have been displaced." DESIGNER: Nishant Jethi LOCATION: Mumbai

TURKISH CARPET This typographic interpretation of a Turkish carpet was designed to train the eye to see and create meaningful images within existing ornamentation. The intricate patterning becomes both letters and digits.
DESIGNER: Mohammed Alhadad
LOCATION: Detroit, MI

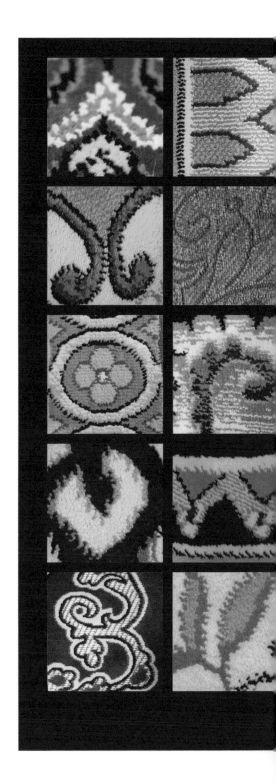

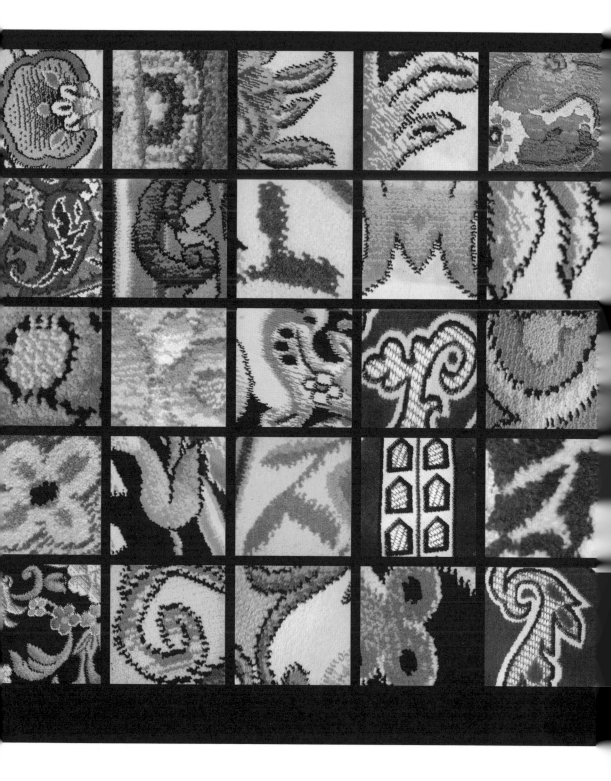

TOZAI TABLES These wooden side tables were inspired by the structural forms of *kanji*, the borrowed or adapted Chinese characters that make up the principal part of the Japanese writing system. They can be read and used either horizontally or as a vertical stack. "*Higashi* (東 – east) and *nishi* (西 – west) form the compound word *tozai* (東西), meaning the wider world." DESIGNERS: Matt Innes, Saori Kajiwara/Device Independent PHOTOGRAPHER: Aaron Walker LOCATION: Melbourne

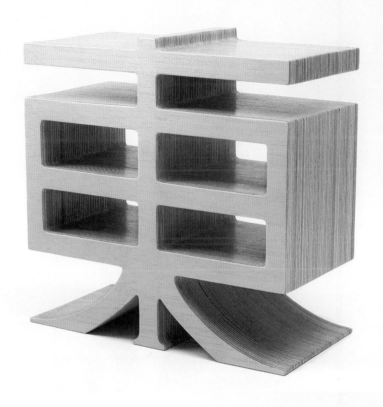

KRAZY KAPS This font was originally designed for a student publication on typography. The typeface was later renamed "Kurlansky's Krazy Kaps" when published in the magazine *U&lc*. DESIGNER: Mervyn Kurlansky/Pentagram CLIENT: Preston Polytechnic LOCATION: London

RUBBER RING "O" While on vacation in Arizona, Xerxes Irani took photographs of letterforms just as he saw them, making sure that no additional manipulation was involved. As he explained: "The only rule was to have no part in creating them." PHOTOGRAPHER: Xerxes Irani LOCATION: Scottsdale, AZ

THE BOOKS SHELF This unique typographic bookshelf, made from jarrah-faced birch ply, holds only the books that one goes back to time and time again. DESIGNERS: Matt Innes, Saori Kajiwara/Device Independent PHOTOGRAPHER: Matt Innes LOCATION: Melbourne

TRASH CAN "U" One unintended consequence of product design is the serendipitous letterform. PHOTOGRAPHER: Gilad Foss LOCATION: New York, NY

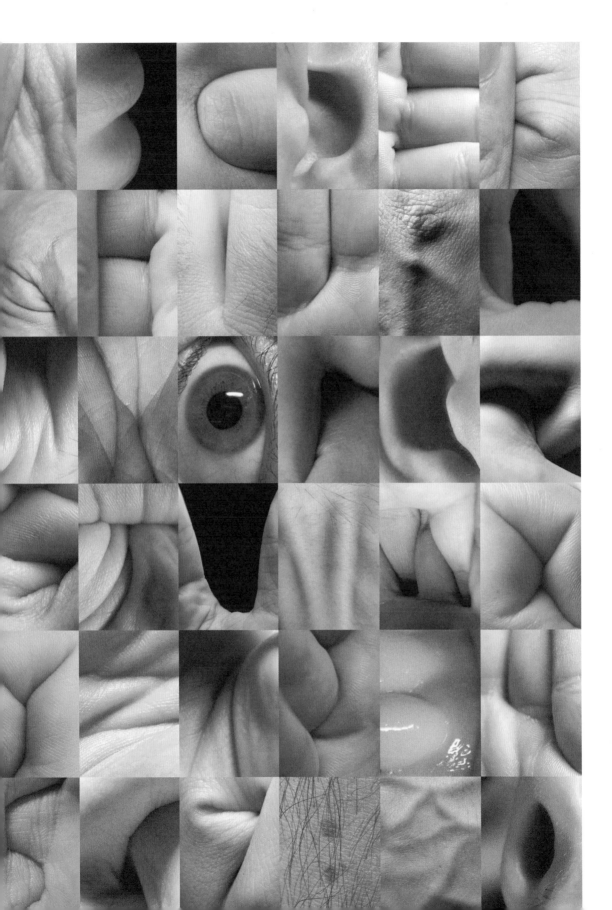

HEADS, LEGS, ARMS, HAIR, AND TOENAILS, TOO

DESIGNING LETTERFORMS FROM EITHER INDIVIDUAL BODY PARTS OR THE entire human body is not as easy as it looks. First, you need a good eye and a steady hand. Some bodily types are so obvious that even Mr Magoo would notice them, while other anatomical letterforms are hiding in plain sight, elusive to the average looker, but not to the seasoned type-spotter. Although it may be easy to focus on finding one, two, or even three letters, building a complete alphabet from fingers, arms, feet, or toes requires a keen imagination.

BODY ALPHABET The designers were asked to find typography in real or animated worlds. "We decided to take a deeper look at the human body," explained Piotr Gajewski. "The final project exceeded our expectations and is full of allusions. The characters are not literal, which encourages the viewer to explore in the search for meaning." PHOTOGRAPHERS: Piotr Gajewski, Grzegorz Samson LOCATION: Gdańsk/Wejherowo, Poland

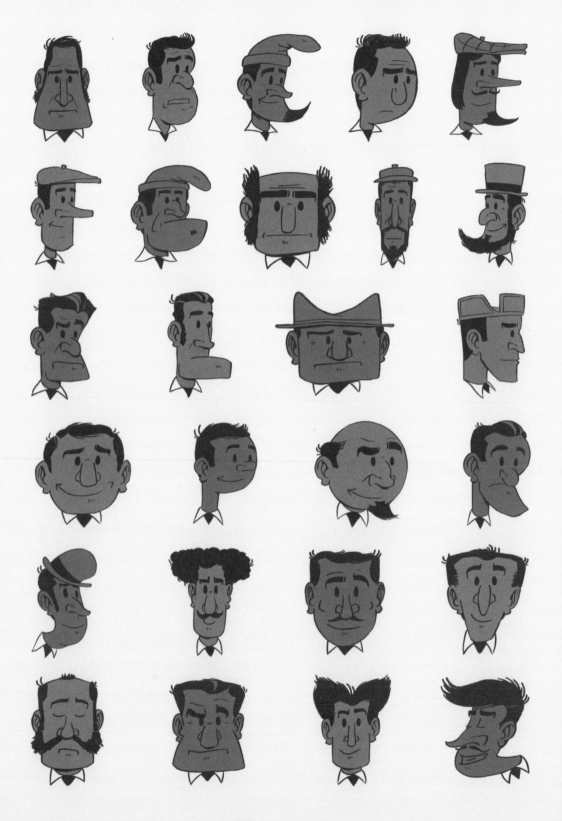

Poisson

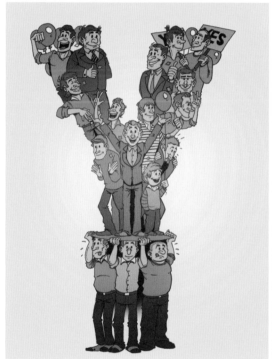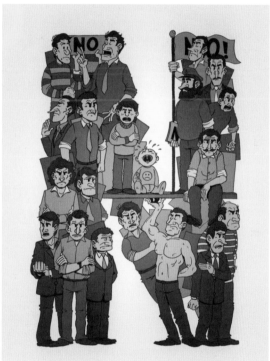

TYPEFACE Julien Poisson created this marriage of illustration and typography as part of a stylistic experiment. ILLUSTRATOR: Julien Poisson LOCATION: Montreal

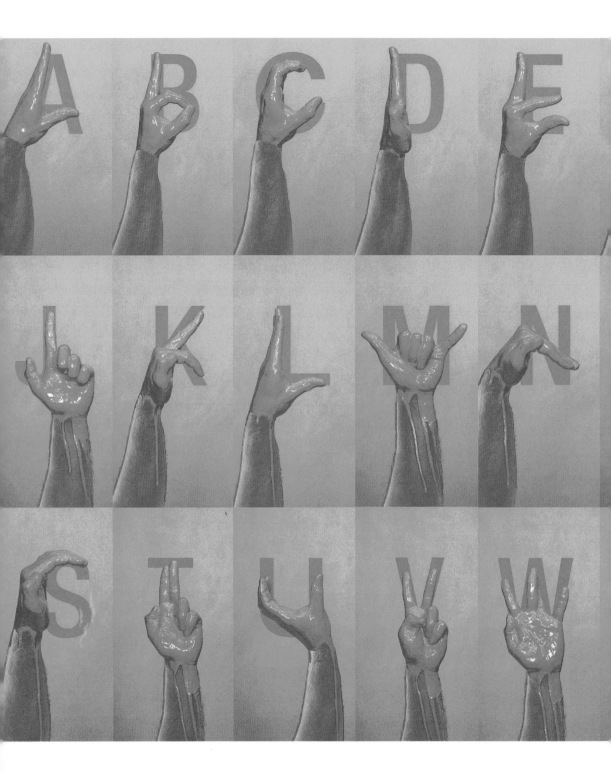

HAND PAINT TYPE The 15th project in a year-long series of typographic experiments collectively titled "Daydreams & Nightschemes" (see pages 123, 256, 262, and 267). Each hand gesture is paired with a letter, creating a series of unexpected hybrid letterforms. The final poster featured the line "Get Your Hands Dirty," a play on the literal and figurative meanings of getting involved in all parts of a job. DESIGNER: Jon Newman PHOTOGRAPHER: Ka Huen Kwong LOCATION: New York, NY

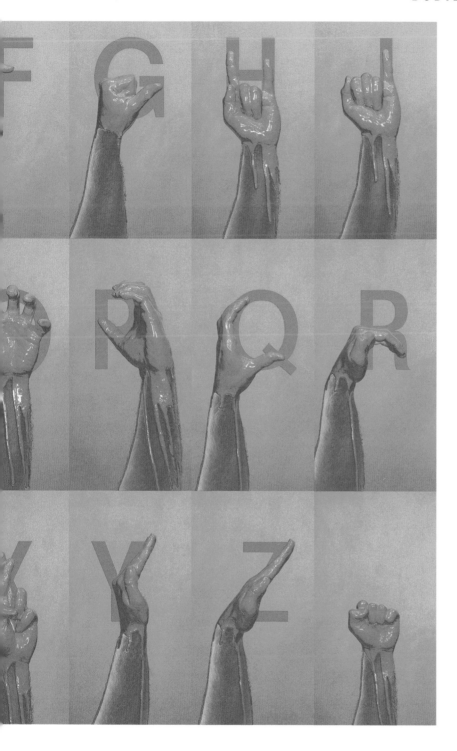

"A" FOR AWESOME / "P" FOR PIRATE Paul
Thurlby designed a pictorial alphabet in a childishly light-
hearted 1950s style. To help young children memorize
the alphabet, he used the basic letter shapes to create
illustrations representing words. (See also page 300.)
ILLUSTRATOR: Paul Thurlby LOCATION: London

for **PIRATE**

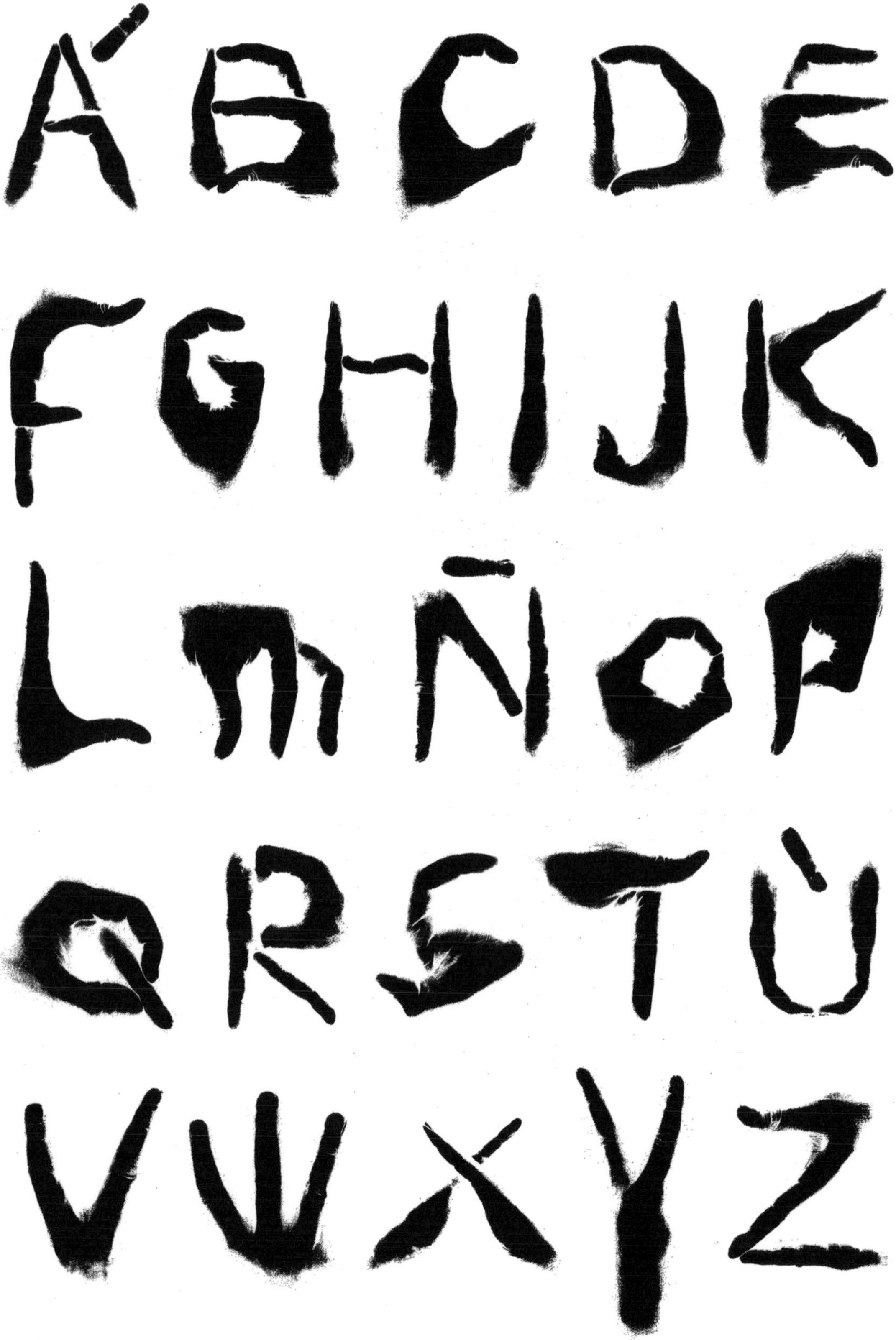
ÁBCDÉ
FGHIJK
LmÑOP
QRSTÙ
VWXYZ

HANDSCHRIFT While sitting in a typography class, José Ernesto Rodríguez played with combinations of "Like hands" (thumbs-up symbols) and exclamation marks, as well as the letters "a," "b," and "c." Later, he tried out his characters by pressing his hand onto the glass of a photocopier to make two-dimensional copies. "After several sometimes painful hand twists and about 400 copies the typeface was completed," he said. "The name of the font is the German word for handwriting." DESIGNER: José Ernesto Rodríguez LOCATION: Berlin

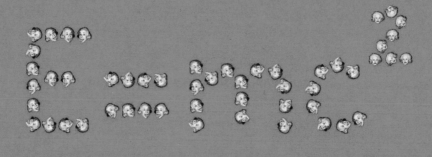

$E = mc^2$ The lettering on this cover design for
Ronald W. Clark's book *Einstein: The Life and
Times* was made from a pointillist array of Einstein
heads. As heady as it was, the design was rejected.
DESIGNER: Robin Bilardello (Photo of Einstein
by Arthur Sasse) CLIENT: Harper Perennial
LOCATION: New York, NY

HANDMADE TYPE Tien-Min Liao
explored the relationship between
upper and lower-case letters,
and recorded the transformation
between them. "I drew shapes with
ink on one or both of my hands,
manipulating my gestures into
the corresponding shape to signify
an upper-case letter. Then…I
manipulated my gesture or changed
the perspective through which
the shape is viewed in order to
transform the upper-case letter into
a lower case of the same letter."
DESIGNER: Tien-Min Liao
LOCATION: New York, NY/Taipei

BALTIMORE LOVE PROJECT: WALL #16 A street-art project initiated by mural artist Michael Owen, whose design of four hands spelling out the word "LOVE" was painted on 20 walls spread evenly across the different areas of the city. "Our mission is to express love by connecting people and communities across Baltimore City through love-themed murals," he explained. Wall #16 is on the site of Baltimore's only city-owned arts center and was completed in September 2012. DESIGNER: Michael Owen PHOTOGRAPHER: Sean Scheidt LOCATION: Baltimore, MD

DANCE WITH ME An alphabet made from 26 carefully choreographed movements.
Dancers traced letter shapes in the air with their hands and arms. Invisible to the
naked eye, the letterforms were captured by long-exposure photography.
DESIGNER: Amandine Alessandra LOCATION: London

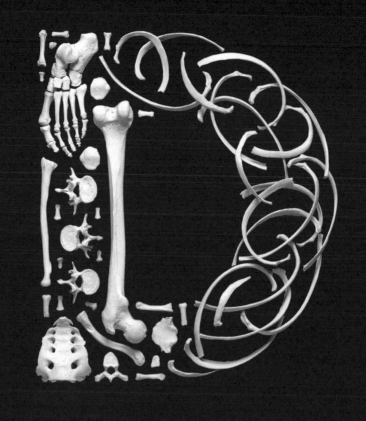
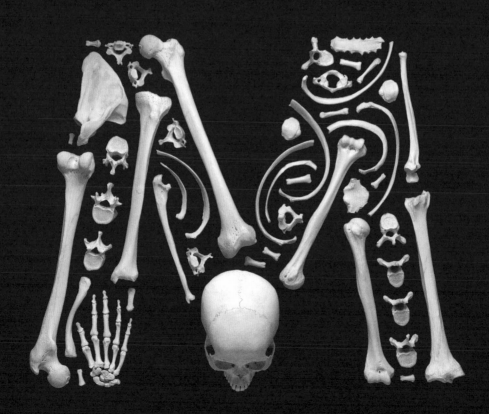

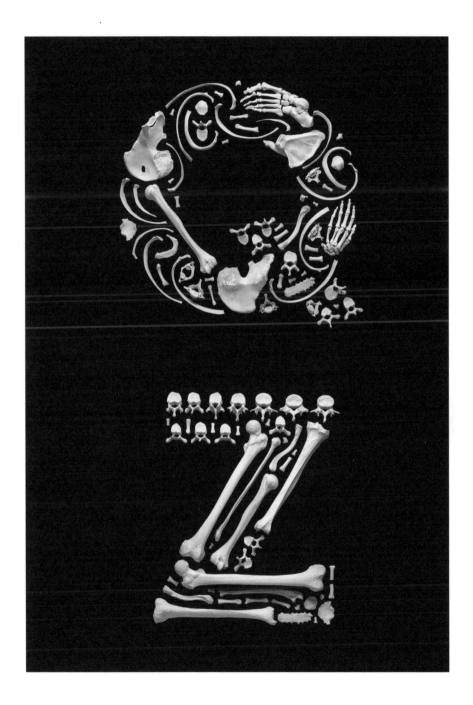

ALPHABONES Francois Robert enjoys taking photographs that "stimulate contemplation and empathy." "I have photographed symbolic objects and cultural signifiers that resonate with the viewer as a statement of the causes and effects of violence," he explains. "Conflict and violence are perpetual areas of focus and concern for human beings. In the end, whatever goals are intended to be achieved by the use of force, the ultimate result is simply the end of life, a dead body." For Robert, the human skeleton is "a powerful visual symbol." Here, he uses all the different bones in the body to form an alphabet that makes a strong statement about the tragedy of war. DESIGNER: Francois Robert/Francois Robert Photography LOCATION: Tucson, AZ © Francois Robert

"L" IN THE SHOWER Believe it or not, this strand of hair on a bathroom wall formed itself naturally into an "L," the first letter of the designer's name. It's more nature than nurture, with a little nudge from water pressure. PHOTOGRAPHER: Louise Fili LOCATION: New York, NY

PRESENT IMPERFECT A project about the play between presence and absence, about something that is there without really being there. "I use hair as a sign of this invisible presence, writing with it emotional or psychic states," said Abril Salas. "The intention is to introduce these words in such common situations as taking a bath, eating, or sleeping." PHOTOGRAPHER: Abril Salas LOCATION: Mexico City

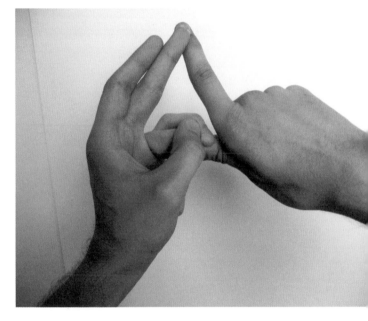

SHADOW TYPE "This started as an exercise in shadow figures and soon got out of hand."
DESIGNER: Kalle Mattsson
LOCATION: Amsterdam

MONEY (THAT'S WHAT I WANT)
For her animation of Barrett Strong's classic Motown single, Camille McMorrow choreographed dancers' movements to create a series of letters that spelled out the lyrics.
DESIGNER: Camille McMorrow
LOCATION: New York, NY

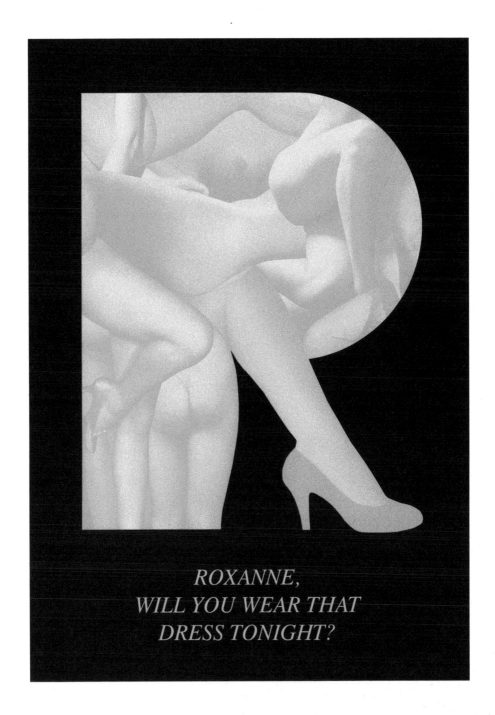

ROXANNE,
WILL YOU WEAR THAT
DRESS TONIGHT?

ROXANNE *Wallpaper** magazine asked a
range of designers to create their own "tart"
cards (signs placed in booths to advertise the
services of prostitutes) in order to highlight
the plight of trafficked women in the sex
industry. DESIGNER: Ahonen & Lamberg
CLIENT: *Wallpaper** LOCATION: Paris

FINGERNAIL TYPE For his experimental typography project "Diary Type" (see pages 38, 42, 112, 128, 280, and 298), Vladimir Končar built this "A" out of his own fingernails, collected over the course of a year.
DESIGNER: Vladimir Končar LOCATION: Zagreb

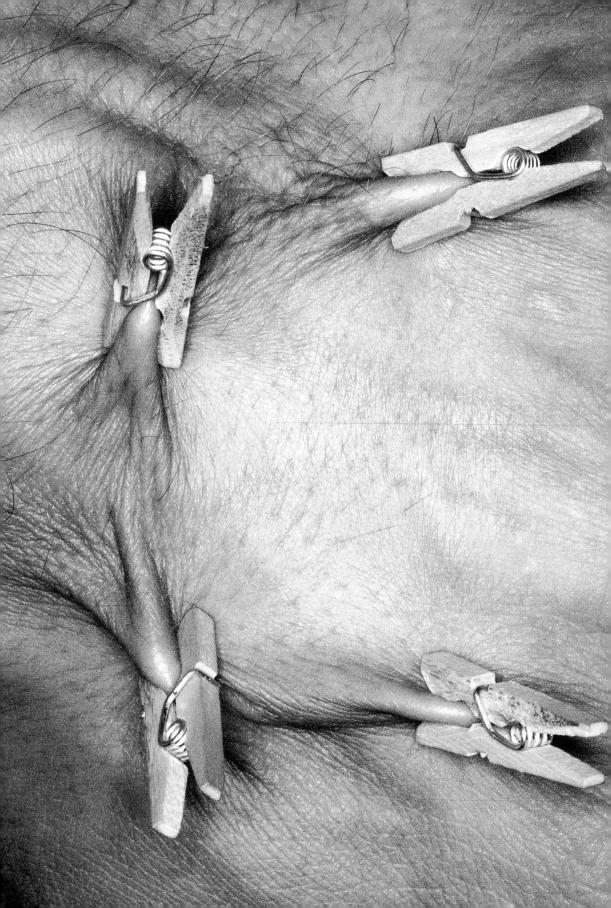

TYPEFACE IN SKIN Each letter in this alphabet, made with clothespins and human skin, has its own unique character thanks to the number of ways in which skin can be pinched and the variety of skin types used. As Thijs Verbeek notes: "Flexible skin results in voluptuous shapes, while tight skin gives the letter a sense of imperfection. This makes it hard to predict the final shape." DESIGNER: Thijs Verbeek PHOTOGRAPHER: Arjan Benning LOCATION: Amsterdam

BACKBREAKER Kalle Mattsson used people and garments to create this "updated version of old engraved letters." DESIGNER: Kalle Mattsson PHOTOGRAPHERS: Tomas Adolfs, Monica Tormell LOCATION: Zaandvoort aan Zee, The Netherlands

BODY TYPE This alphabet experiments with the letterforms that emerge when the human body is bent or stretched into different shapes. It plays on the similarities between typesetting terminology and the vocabulary used to describe the body: anatomy, body size, headpiece, footer, leg, eye, arms, chin, hairline, etc. DESIGNER: Amandine Alessandra LOCATION: London

SPUIPLEIN LETTERS While working for the communication agency Vandejong in Amsterdam, Kalle Mattsson developed a new design identity for the cultural center Spuiplein in The Hague, which is home to that city's resident orchestra and the Dutch Dance Theater. "For the basic elements in the campaign I made a system to order the material and a series of letters to use in the program and catalog," she said. DESIGNER: Kalle Mattsson/Vandejong CLIENT: Spuiplein LOCATION: Amsterdam/The Hague

GOURMET AND GOURMAND LETTERING

TYPOGRAPHY DOES NOT USE UP ANY AIR OR TAKE UP MUCH SPACE IN OUR FRAGILE environment, unless one counts all the paper it is printed on, all the trees cut down to make that paper, and all the chemical waste produced by this process. Still, type itself, especially digital type, is self-sustaining. But now there's "green type" – letterforms made from nature's bounty, from flora and fauna. Most solid food can be manipulated and contorted into alphabets and words, while other foodstuffs are just naturally alphabetic. Is there anything more sublime than a font set made of artichoke hearts, or other fruits and veggies? This chapter is a tempting feast of fresh and natural typographic wonders created from avocados, tomatoes, passion fruit, and more.

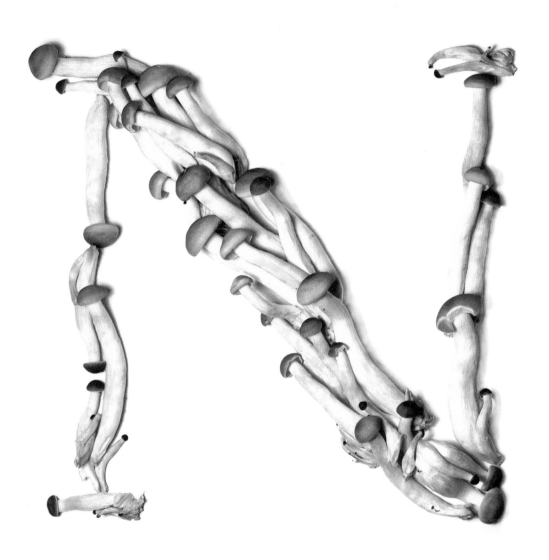

MUSHROOM CAP This "N" is from a series of initial caps made from different types of mushrooms. It was inspired by the TEDtalk "My Mushroom Burial Suit" by Jae Rhim Lee, in which the artist proposed a way for humans to commit their bodies to a greener earth, even after death. DESIGNER: Nari Park ART DIRECTOR: Barbara DeWilde LOCATION: New York, NY

WILD AT HEART Camille McMorrow's delicate response to a design assignment that instructed students to create type from something "inside." "I enjoyed the way artichoke hearts took on very human characteristics, almost like bones, joints, and fibers, and the way they speak to the human forms that exist in type," she said. DESIGNER: Camille McMorrow LOCATION: New York, NY

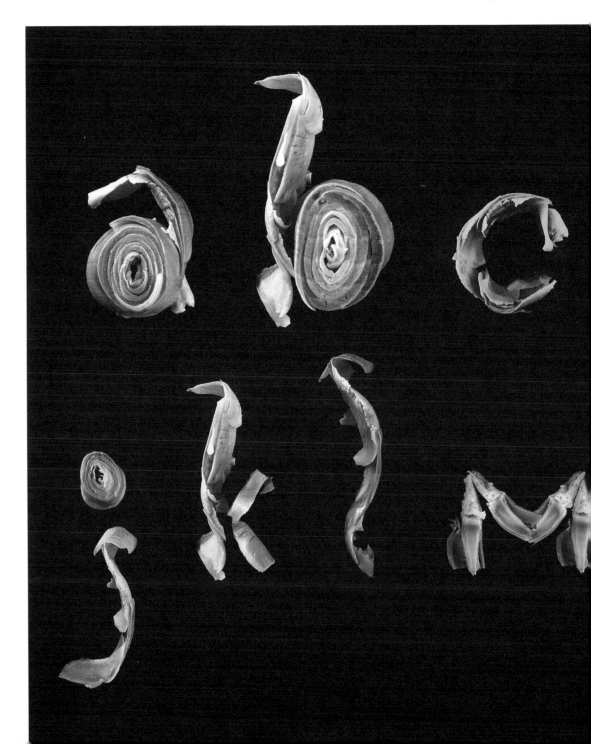

YUM This mouth-watering project started out as an entry for Ethan Bodnar's design inspiration book *Creative Crab Bag*. The brief was to represent all or any of the senses.
DESIGNER: Paul Stonier
LOCATION: Elmira, NY

FRUITS & VEGGIES A colorful alphabet celebrating the variety of organic lines and forms in fresh produce. It's amazing just what can be found in nature's own. PHOTOGRAPHER: Irina Wang LOCATION: Florida

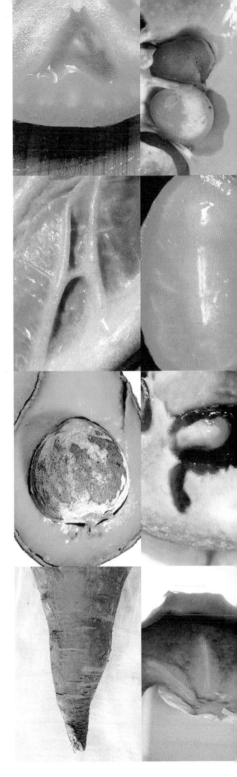

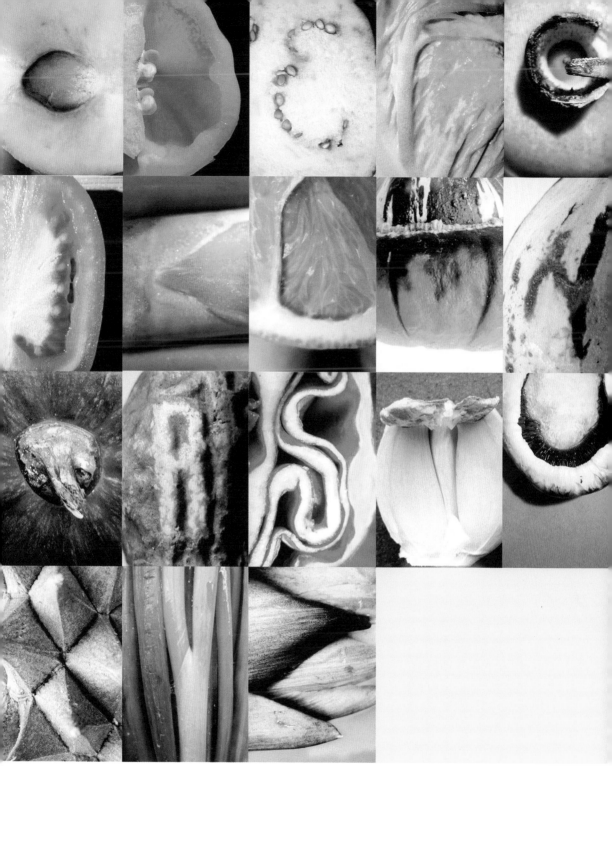

BEAN TYPE A lower-case "g" formed out of white beans as part of Vladimir Končar's experimental "Diary Type" series (see pages 38, 42, 101, 128, 280, and 298).
DESIGNER: Vladimir Končar
LOCATION: Zagreb

RUE LA LA These designs for the monthly newsletter of a member's-only online fashion boutique brought the company's eclectic vision to life.
DESIGNER: Saddington Baynes
PHOTOGRAPHER: Joshua Delsimer
CLIENT: Rue La La
LOCATION: New York, NY

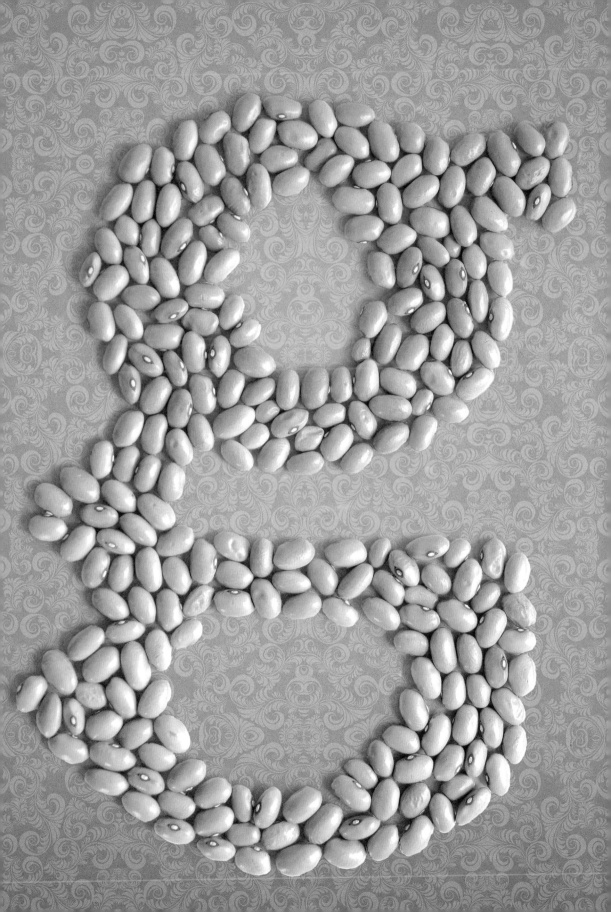

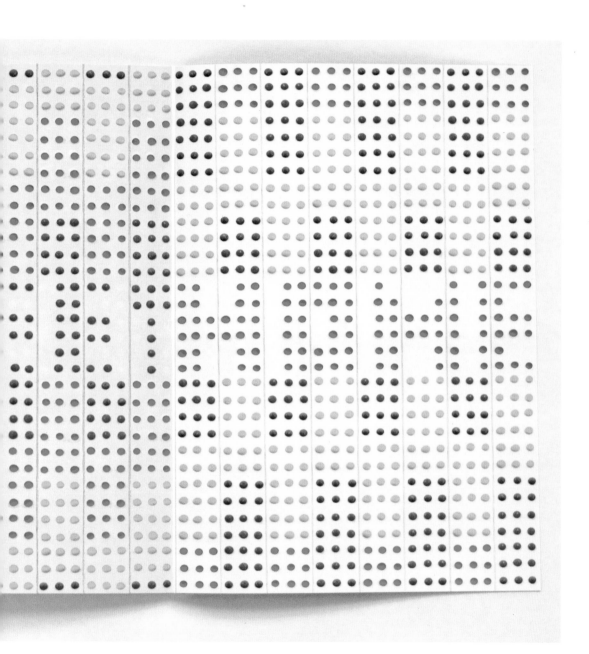

CANDY BUTTONS This centerfold feature from the second issue of design magazine *Gratuitous Type* was inspired by candy buttons. "Four perforated peel-away strips invite readers to reveal a secret panel that changes the tone of the nostalgic childhood treat," Mark Pernice explained. "The adhered strips are even replaceable."
DESIGNER: Mark Pernice PHOTOGRAPHER: Ross Mantle ILLUSTRATORS: Ashley Nodar, Wing Chui
ART DIRECTORS: Elana Schlenker, Mark Pernice CLIENT: *Gratuitous Type* LOCATION: New York, NY

DORITOS "I love these chips!" said José Ernesto Rodríguez of his tasty, carb-filled alphabet. DESIGNER: José Ernesto Rodríguez LOCATION: Bournemouth, UK

ANYONE FOR TEA Based on a report by the anti-poverty charity War on Want, this advertisement used tea leaves to spell out a message highlighting the exploitation of tea workers in India and Kenya. DESIGNER: Patrick Knowles LOCATION: London

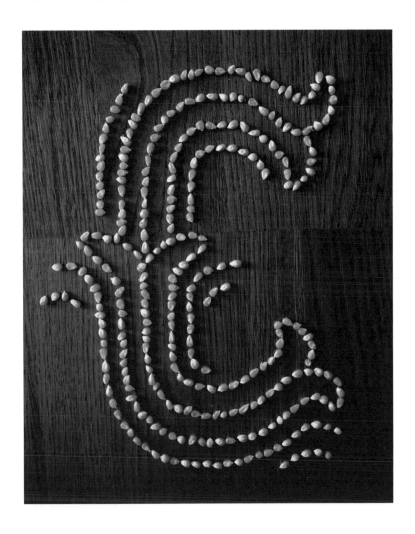

BEAUTIFUL BITMAPS A "C" made of kernels of corn from *Uppercase*'s "Beautiful Bitmaps" issue. The magazine invited 20 designers, illustrators, and typographers to build letters out of individual elements, either digital or physical. DESIGNER: Ryan Feerer CLIENT: *Uppercase* LOCATION: Abilene, TX

HAPPY! Part of a handmade typography experiment on happiness. "Eating enough carbohydrates can make you happy," noted Vladimir Končar. DESIGNER: Vladimir Končar LOCATION: Zagreb

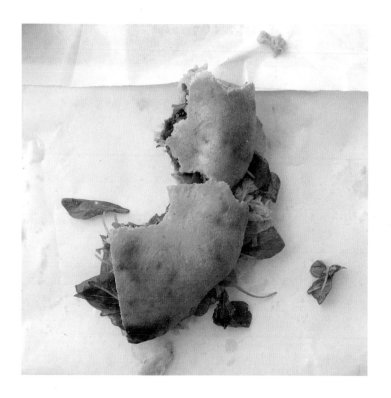

"J" ON A ROLL While on holiday in Arizona,
Xerxes Irani spotted this "J" in a half-eaten sandwich.
PHOTOGRAPHER: Xerxes Irani LOCATION: Scottsdale, AZ

VEGGIE SPREAD "Our busy lifestyles and the abundance of fast food
lead to people neglecting their health," explained Stephy Chee. This
project "highlights the importance and benefits of eating fresh fruits and
vegetables. Make every meal healthier, because you are what we eat."
DESIGNER: Stephy Chee LOCATION: Malaysia

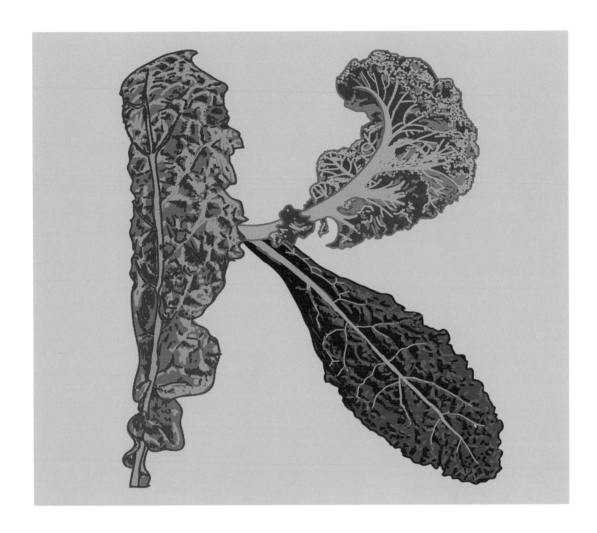

VITAMIN KALE In 2013, Jen Montgomery posted
a new illustration on her website on a weekly basis
in order to keep current. This design was inspired by
"the amazing energy I was getting from kale shakes,"
she explained. ILLUSTRATOR: Jen Montgomery
LOCATION: Los Angeles, CA

POURED MILK FONT
For the 24th project
in his "Daydreams &
Nightschemes" series (see
pages 82, 256, 262, and
267), Jon Newman poured
milk through hand-cut
black plastic cups to
reveal letterforms. He was
inspired by "the energetic
motion of a waterfall."
DESIGNER: Jon Newman
PHOTOGRAPHER:
Ka Huen Kwong
LOCATION:
New York, NY

LOVE CHIPS Everyone loves fried potatoes. Taking as her starting-point Robert Indiana's iconic Pop-art *LOVE*, a design reproduced in sculptural form in cities across the globe, Sónia Lamêra cooked up a tempting typographic delight.
DESIGNER: Sónia Lamêra
LOCATION: Lisbon

MENGEM (EAT) More object lettering created by Mòn Castel for a fictitious magazine with the aim of helping children to "discover the world around them through interesting pictures and topics." DESIGNER: Mòn Castel LOCATION: Barcelona

CHICKEN SKIN Now we know why the chicken crossed the road. This experimental epidermal lettering was made by hand from parts of raw chicken. DESIGNER: Rui Lira LOCATION: Amsterdam

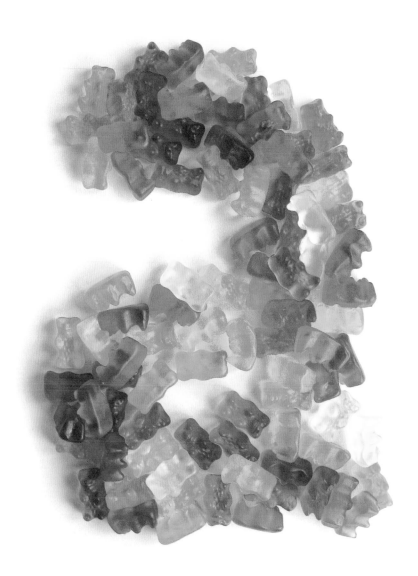

GUMMY BEAR TYPE This soft candy typeface was another project in Vladimir Končar's eclectic series "Diary Type" (see pages 38, 42, 101, 112, 280, and 298). DESIGNER: Vladimir Končar LOCATION: Zagreb

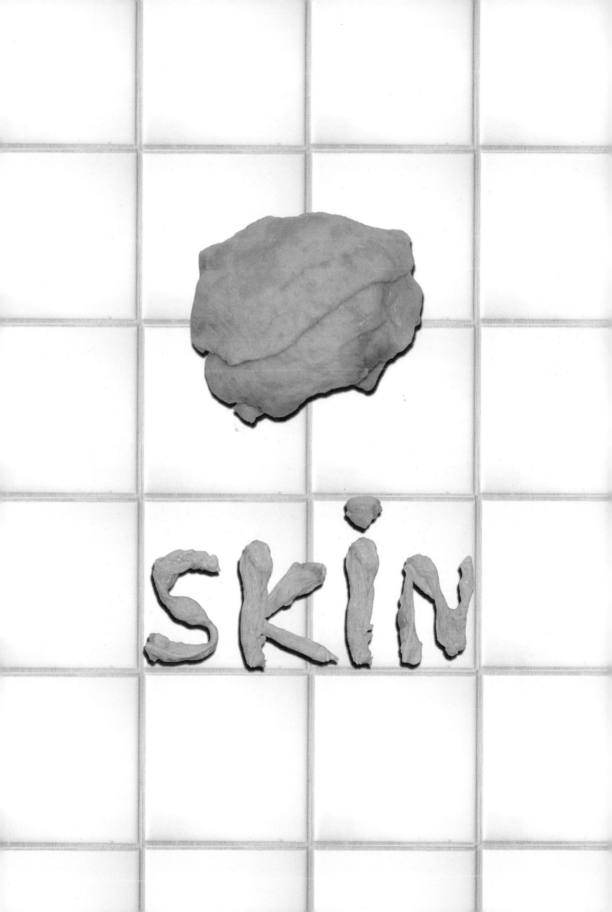

ENTDECKE, WAS DIR SCHMECKT (DISCOVER WHAT TASTES GOOD)
Chapter dividers from a children's cookbook that not only contains recipes and
practical kitchen advice, but also helps kids to discover what they like to eat and
why. The typography is made from the ingredients discussed in the subsequent pages.
DESIGNER: Lisa Rienermann CLIENT: Beltz & Gelberg LOCATION: Berlin

Wie kaufe ich schlau ein?

AN END TO ALL THINGS The cover of a story collection by Jared Yates Sexton. The spilled milk design encapsulates the themes of turmoil, tension, and chaos described philosophically in the stories, but in an everyday kind of way. DESIGNER: Jamie Keenan CLIENT: Atticus Books LOCATION: London

FINGERHOT PEPPER FONT "I chose to create a font using these peppers," explained Laura C. Temple, "because they have the three elements of a letter: straight lines, diagonals, and curves. There would be no need for photo manipulation." DESIGNER: Laura C. Temple ART DIRECTOR: Kimberly Elam LOCATION: Sarasota, FL

an end to all things

Jared Yates Sexton

POMEGRANATE More accidental lettering spotted in New
York during a student exercise in typographic observation.
PHOTOGRAPHER: Najeebah Al-Ghadban
LOCATION: New York, NY

PARMESAN "V" The pungent "V" from a collection of photographs
of unintentional letterforms. PHOTOGRAPHER: Emily Engelson
LOCATION: New York, NY

MACHINE-AGE LETTERING

SOMETIMES TYPEFACES APPEAR SERENDIPITOUSLY IN THE PIPES, DUCTS, AND gears of machinery, but they can also be built from these contraptions. Industrial letterforms are often bigger than the average types, yet occasionally come on a smaller scale. The vast variety of geometric forms that fall into this category range from the blatantly obvious to the wittily obscure. If you look hard enough, you'll find letters and ligatures in railings, wheels, metal grates, and more. It makes one wonder whether the creators of these structures were aware of what the eagle-eyed type maven can see.

FOUND TYPE EXPLORATIONS Type is everywhere on the streets of St Petersburg. PHOTOGRAPHER: Nadya Rodionenko LOCATION: St Petersburg

THE NUMBER HOUSE Ready-built homes such as these are often mass-produced and developed on a large scale, resulting in entire rows of generic housing units. "In many cases," explain the architect, "the appearance is coordinated at the designation of the owner and rows of houses that do not necessarily match aesthetically are created." The owner of these particular blocks wanted a sense of unity. By turning the otherwise commonplace balconies into numbers, the four units appear as one building. DESIGNER: Mitsutomo Matsunami Architects LOCATION: Osaka, Japan

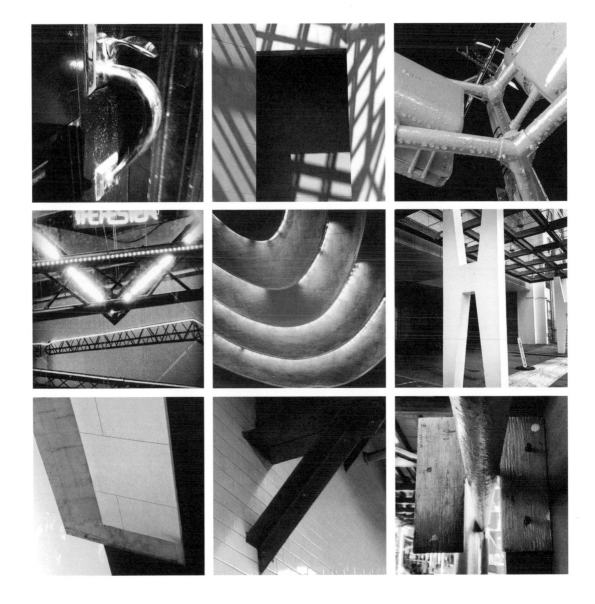

ABCDEVERYWHERE A range of industrial letterforms found and captured in various urban locations. PHOTOGRAPHER: Zipeng Zhu LOCATION: New York, NY

"X" MARKS THE SPOT This photograph was taken on Chicago's North Avenue Beach in summer 2013. PHOTOGRAPHER: Jane Robert/Francois Robert Photography LOCATION: Chicago, IL © Francois Robert

MUSEUM "V" While visiting Budapest, Abigail Steinem fell in love with the city: "Everything in Budapest is beautiful, even the air vents." She found this "V" in the Museum of Applied Arts, an Art Nouveau building completed in 1896. PHOTOGRAPHER: Abigail Steinem LOCATION: Budapest

ALPHABET TRUCK These photographs of letters on the backs of trucks represent several thousands of miles traveled. Through language (the letters) and displacement (the trucks), the series of images looks "beyond its formal aspects and references" to question "notions of membership, identity, and cultural diversity." PHOTOGRAPHER: Eric Tabuchi CLIENT: Florence Loewy LOCATION: France

ABC TRASH Building an alphabet out of trash and other discarded objects is a bit like curating an archaeological dig. The found items were displayed on four large wooden panels. DESIGNER: Fabio De Minicis LOCATION: Barcelona

LOOK DOWN, WHAT DO YOU SEE? The streets of the Bushwick neighborhood of Brooklyn are filled with lettering, it's just a matter of looking in the right place at the right time. PHOTOGRAPHER: Eivor Pedersen LOCATION: Bushwick, Brooklyn, NY

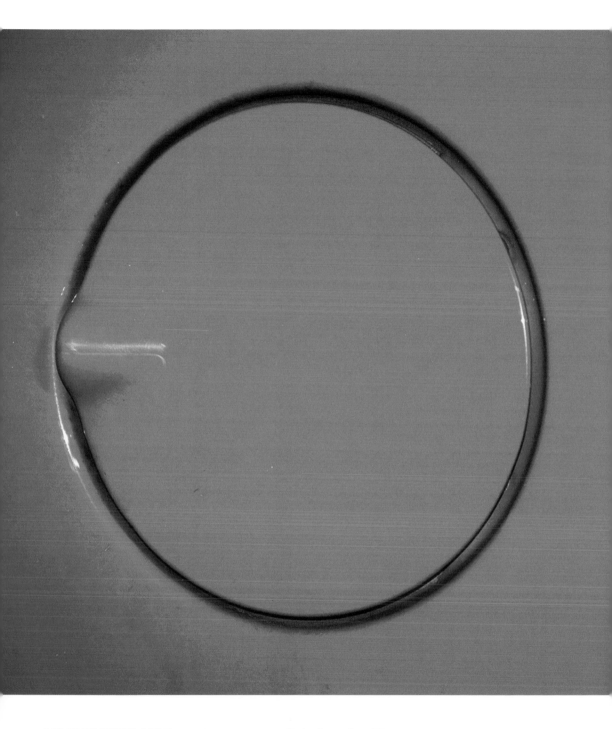

GAS TANK COVER "O" For a junior-year project at Pennsylvania State University, Julie Wuenschel and her classmates were given a different letter, number, and symbol to find in the everyday environment. PHOTOGRAPHER: Julie Wuenschel ART DIRECTOR: Kristin Sommese LOCATION: State College, PA

FIRE ESCAPE "Z" What could be more perfect than the "Z" shape formed by the zigzag of a fire escape? PHOTOGRAPHER: Marjorie Lin LOCATION: New York, NY

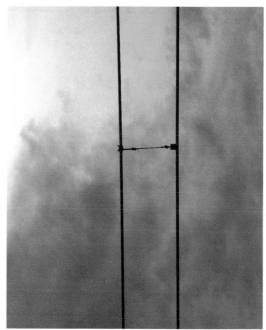

**WOOD, DOORKNOBS, RAILTRACKS &
POWER LINES** When you zoom in on certain
objects and structures, letters appear before your
very eyes. PHOTOGRAPHER: Emily Engelson
LOCATION: New York, NY

**RAILINGS &
DOORHANDLES**
More letters formed
by city details.
PHOTOGRAPHER:
Reham Ibrahim
LOCATION:
New York, NY

SPIGOTS, PIPES, DUCTS & HANDLES
Further examples of found lettering from a
student exercise on typographic perception.
PHOTOGRAPHER: Felipe Garcia
LOCATION: New York, NY

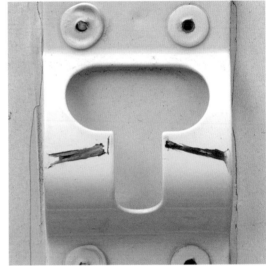

METAL "I" Iron on exposed brick leaves a Brutalist typographic impression. PHOTOGRAPHER: Manasrawee Nham Wongpradu LOCATION: Astoria, Queens, NY

BINS, RAILINGS & LIGHT BULBS There are endless possibilities of serendipitous urban lettering. PHOTOGRAPHER: Gilad Foss LOCATION: New York, NY

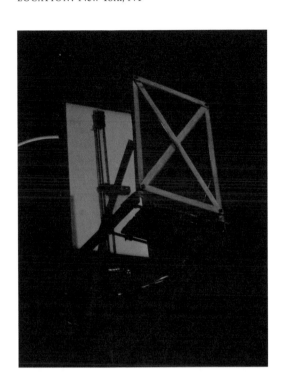

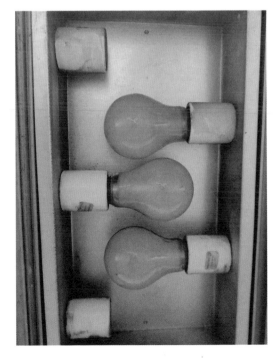

DUCT "Y" Even an innocuous heat duct can produce an elegant "Y."
PHOTOGRAPHER: Kenny Batu LOCATION: New York, NY

GRATE "C" More letters formed quite naturally
by urban architecture and nature. PHOTOGRAPHER:
Thomas Strobel LOCATION: New York, NY

PEEPHOLE "8" With its cover raised, this small eyehole turns into an "8." PHOTOGRAPHER: Sasha Prood LOCATION: Brooklyn, NY

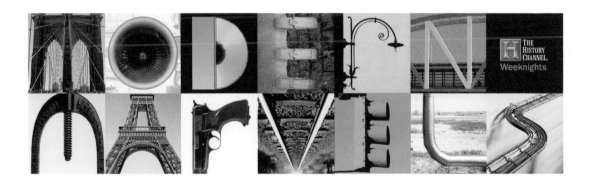

MODERN MARVELS Billboard advertising for the History Channel's long-running series on design. Photographs of iconic inventions and constructions were used to create letters that spelled out the title of the show. DESIGNER: Graham Clifford Design PHOTOGRAPHER: Peter Cunningham ART DIRECTOR: Callum MacGregor LOCATION: New York, NY

LONDON ALPHABET A full A to Z of objects found on London streets. PHOTOGRAPHER: Dan Page/ The Creative Arms ART DIRECTORS: Craig Brooks, Jamie Rankin LOCATION: London

GAPING "O" This photograph was taken on a trip to Paris in 2013. PHOTOGRAPHER: Jane Robert/Francois Robert Photography LOCATION: Paris © Francois Robert

URBAN ALPHABET For this assignment, part of the Cornell University course "Making a Difference by Design," students were asked to look at their environments afresh. These letterforms are the result of careful observation. PHOTOGRAPHER: Emelia Day LOCATION: Ithaca, NY

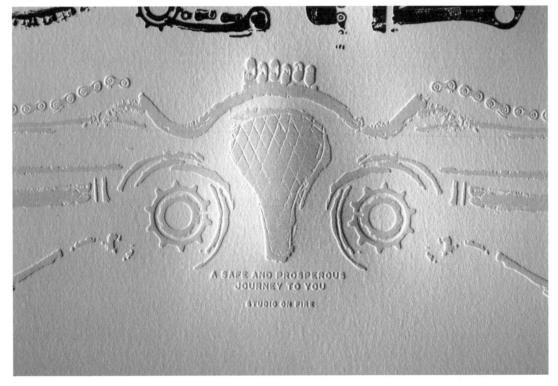

A SAFE AND PROSPEROUS
JOURNEY TO YOU

STUDIO ON FIRE

GODSPEED A composition designed in 2011 for Artcrank, a "poster party for bike people." The assemblage was created with actual bicycle parts inked up with a brayer and then letterpress printed by hand. "We printed all kinds of parts: cranks, chains, cables, wheels, handlebars, and even a seat," explained the Studio On Fire crew. "It was amazing how much type and texture come out of each part. These prints were then digitally arranged on top of a pencil-sketched layout. The word 'Godspeed' seems especially appropriate for cyclists, as a wish for someone's safe and prosperous journey." DESIGNER: Studio On Fire CLIENT: Artcrank LOCATION: Minneapolis, MN

MONOGRAM Holes gouged into a piece of metal
become a personalized monogram for an unknown farmer.
PHOTOGRAPHER: Jane Robert/Francois Robert Photography
LOCATION: Park City, UT © Francois Robert

DOTS Splotchy letters hastily daubed on a
wall commemorate another mystery person.
PHOTOGRAPHER: Carin Goldberg
LOCATION: Paris

GOOK "U" Even muck on the street can form the shape of a letter, or even a smile. PHOTOGRAPHER: Xerxes Irani LOCATION: Scottsdale, AZ

PAINTED "X" A red "X" scrawled on a simple wooden garage gate in a small seaside town. PHOTOGRAPHER: Erica Jung/ PintassilgoPrints LOCATION: Guarapari, Brazil

XEROX Decay transforms this ordinary type into extraordinary lettering. Although almost unreadable, it's certainly attention grabbing. PHOTOGRAPHER: Erica Jung/ PintassilgoPrints LOCATION: Guarapari, Brazil

DISCOMFORT For his *San Francisco* painting series, Pablo A. Medina paid homage to vernacular street signage, borrowing the formats of the original signs but substituting in his own messages. DESIGNER: Pablo A. Medina LOCATION: San Francisco, CA

WOBBLY "O" Black paint on a ridged white surface conjures up alphabetic imagery.
PHOTOGRAPHER: Jane Robert/Francois Robert Photography LOCATION: Paris © Francois Robert

CORRUGATED "X" Corrugated metal siding defines
the style of this letter. PHOTOGRAPHER: Carin Goldberg
LOCATION: Paris

BOLT Thanks to its neon color and the startling seductiveness of the positioning of the tape, this lettering on a busy shopping street instantly caught the attention of the photographer.
PHOTOGRAPHER: Abigail Steinem LOCATION: Budapest

LONGING Pablo A. Medina creates images based on hand-painted signage, replacing the original text with his own, more poetic messages. This painting is from his *New York* series.
DESIGNER: Pablo A. Medina
LOCATION: New York, NY

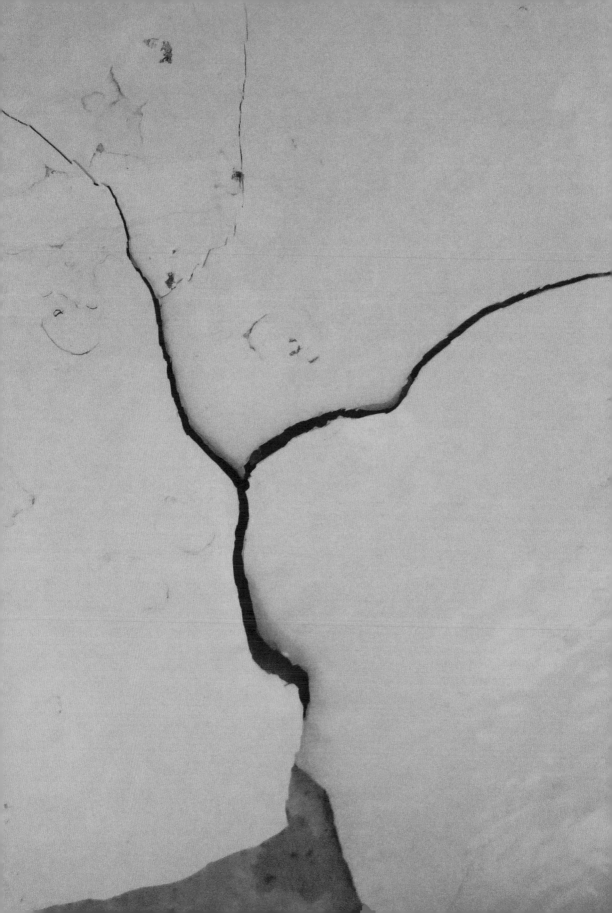

CRACKED PAINT "Y" Cracks in old painted walls often create surprising shapes and letters. PHOTOGRAPHER: Gilad Foss LOCATION: New York, NY

MOLDING "T" Wooden wall molding forms the rectilinear "T" in this New York-based alphabet. PHOTOGRAPHER: Eren Su Kibele Yarman LOCATION: New York, NY

CORRUGATED NUMBER "1" Is this shape a "1" or something else? Its charm lies in its ambiguity. PHOTOGRAPHER: Carin Goldberg LOCATION: Paris

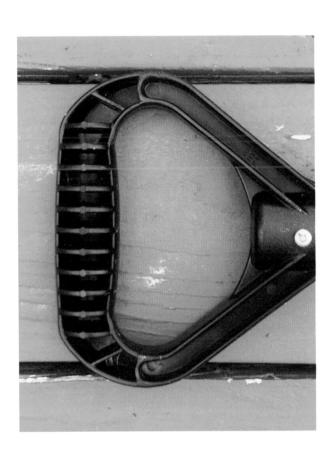

HANDLE "D" This plastic "D" really sneaks up on the viewer.
PHOTOGRAPHER: Emily Engelson LOCATION: New York, NY

STREET-SMART LETTERING

T HE GREAT OUTDOORS, BE IT URBAN OR RURAL, IS A
typographic hornet's nest. If you get too close the letters will disappear,
but don't stand too far away either. All around us are shapes and objects,
both man-made and natural, that are ripe for type-casting; the earth
and heavens are full of signs, marks, scratches, and scrawls that inspire
typographic recognition. Look down and you'll find letters in reflective
traffic markings, then look up and you'll see criss-crossed airplane vapor
trails turning into unintentional skywriting. While some of these letterforms cry out to the passer-by, others require us to contort our heads
and strain our eyes before they finally emerge. You might say that type
is in the eye of the beholder.

NO STOPPING ZONE Ceol Ryder created this confabulation by painstakingly
photographing sections of a yellow street grid from various different angles.
"I got a lot of strange looks from people passing by," he recalled with a grin.
DESIGNER: Ceol Ryder LOCATION: Limerick, Ireland

A B C D

F G H I

L O O P

R S T U V

X Y

STOP A constant stream of traffic and the beat of the sun's rays conspired to turn this commonplace "STOP" lettering into an expressionistic glyph.
PHOTOGRAPHER: Jane Robert/Francois Robert Photography
LOCATION: Reykjavik © Francois Robert

ABC CHEMTRAILS An alphabet made from photographs of airplane vapor trails. PHOTOGRAPHER: Fabio De Minicis LOCATION: Barcelona

FARMYARD TYPE How many letters are in this gaggle of outdoor objects found on a Swiss farm? PHOTOGRAPHER: Jane Robert/Francois Robert Photography LOCATION: Switzerland © Francois Robert

ARIZONA SHAPES More fortuitous letterforms discovered in situ during a trip to Arizona. PHOTOGRAPHER: Xerxes Irani LOCATION: Scottsdale, AZ

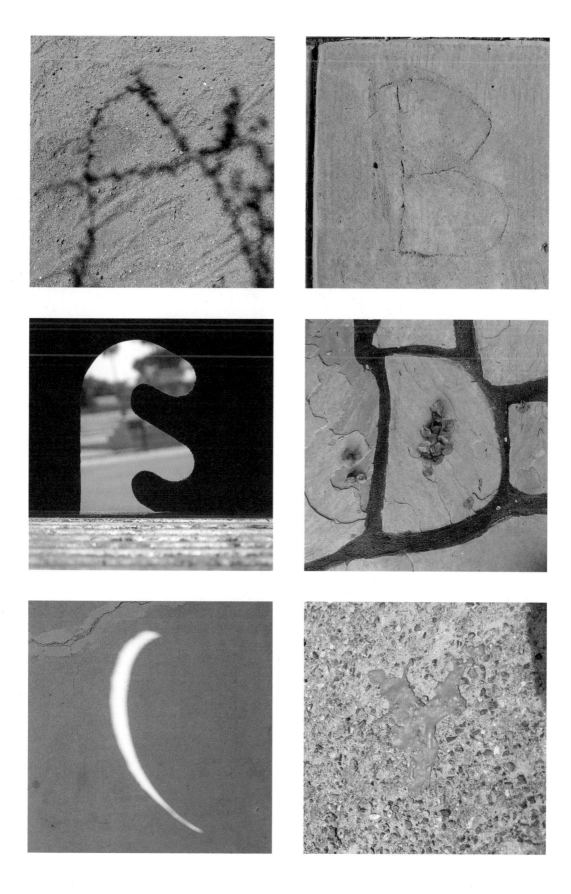

"B" IS FOR BERRIES For her book *The Natural Alphabet*, Susan Klim photographed letterforms spotted in trees and on the ground during daily dog walks through New York's Central Park. She then paired the photographs with images of natural objects also found in the park and starting with the same letter. PHOTOGRAPHER: Susan Klim LOCATION: New York, NY

ABCDEVERYWHERE The tarpaulin "I" from Zipeng Zhu's
"Everywhere" alphabet. PHOTOGRAPHER: Zipeng Zhu
LOCATION: New York, NY

GOOGLE SEARCH "Over the course of six months, I spent some of my spare time between commercial projects searching Google Maps, hoping to discover land formations or buildings resembling letterforms," said Rhett Dashwood. "These are the results of my findings, limited within the state of Victoria." DESIGNER: Rhett Dashwood LOCATION: Victoria, Australia

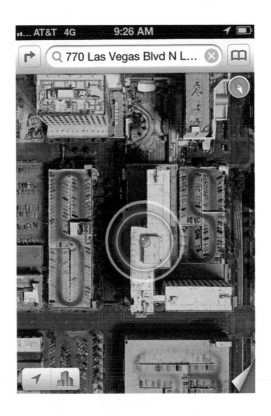

LAS VEGAS DISTRESS SIGNAL Jonathan Parker was using his iPhone's Apple Maps application to navigate the Fremont Street district of Las Vegas when he noticed these "S"-shaped wear patterns on the top floors of parking garages. "I realized that the circular location indicator would create an 'O,' so I walked through the hotel to position myself just so, then took a screen capture when it looked like 'SOS.'" DESIGNER: Jonathan Parker LOCATION: Las Vegas, NV

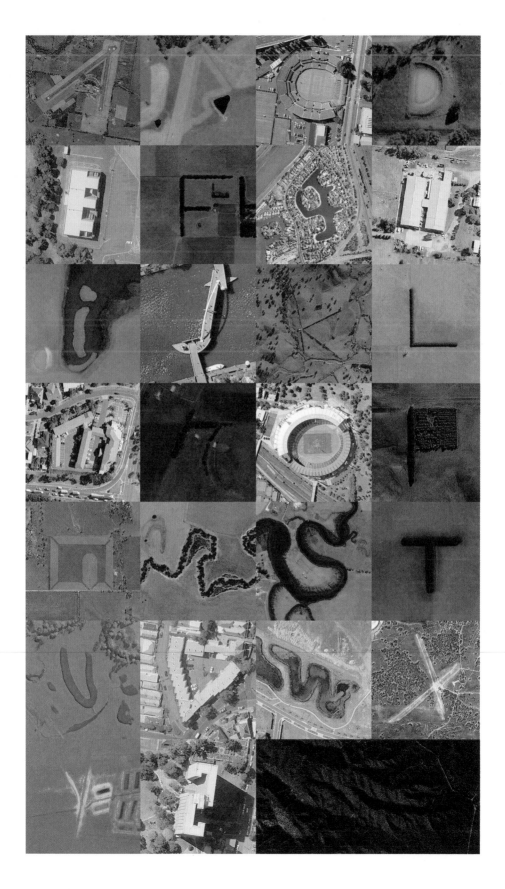

TRAILS IN THE SKY Wherever there are airplanes, there are letters forming in the open sky. PHOTOGRAPHER: Eivor Pedersen LOCATION: Kristiansand, Norway

LOWER EAST SIDE "F" A lamp post becomes a slender "F" on this bustling city street. PHOTOGRAPHER: Patricia Sánchez Navarro LOCATION: New York, NY

ROAD MARKING "V" Letters on the asphalt in the Lower
East Side. PHOTOGRAPHER: Patricia Sánchez Navarro
LOCATION: New York, NY

FLATIRON TYPE Look at this iconic building one
way and it turns into a "V." The next second, it becomes
an "I." PHOTOGRAPHER: Mohammad Sharaf
LOCATION: New York, NY

TAI LONG SAI WAN The construction of a large private residence directly behind this beach in the upper Sai Wan Village promises to destroy the sandy shore, one of the most beautiful coastlines in Hong Kong. Using only sea water and sand, this experimental typography project aims to inspire Hong Kong citizens to experience nature and cherish their environment. DESIGNER: Jim Wong/Good Morning LOCATION: Hong Kong

LETTERING TREE This tree trunk, carefully carved with all kinds of messages, was found in Michigan's Warren Woods.
PHOTOGRAPHER: Francois Robert/ Francois Robert Photography
LOCATION: Warren Woods, MI
© Francois Robert

PAVING STONE "K" Many European streets are paved with uneven cobblestones or rough-cut slabs. This shape was of particular interest to Abigail Steinem. "The only time I saw it was outside the Central Market Hall, which is Budapest's main produce market," she recalled.
PHOTOGRAPHER: Abigail Steinem LOCATION: Budapest

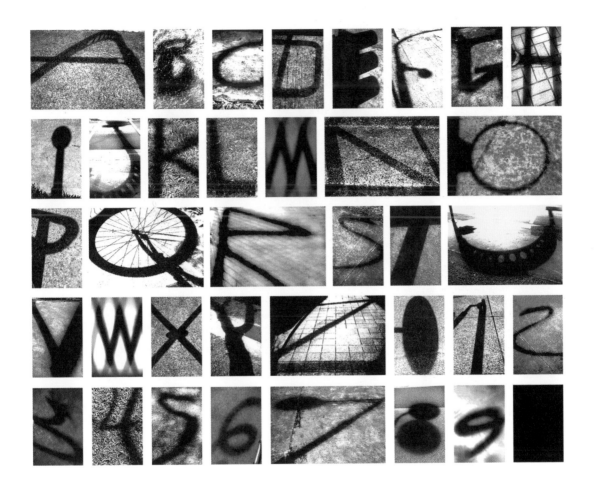

INCIDENTALS These photographs were taken in Singapore for a project that aimed "to change our perspective of shadows from boring to interesting."
PHOTOGRAPHER: Ammanda Choo LOCATION: Singapore

A, B, SEE – 1, 2, THREE To describe his degree project, a series of photographs of typographic tree forms, Christian Brandt poetically quoted Shakespeare's *Antony and Cleopatra*: "Sometimes we see a cloud that's dragonish, / A vapor sometime like a bear or lion, / A towered citadel, a pendant rock, / A forked mountain, or blue promontory / With trees upon 't, that nod unto the world / And mock our eyes with air…" PHOTOGRAPHER: Christian Brandt LOCATION: Stockholm

SIDEWALK TYPE Is this an "X," a "Y," or an "A"? Spindly shadow letters spotted on the city streets.
PHOTOGRAPHER: Muddyum LOCATION: Brooklyn, NY

FOAM "C" A crushed Styrofoam clamshell may be environmentally abominable, but it does make an great "C" in Najeebah Al-Ghadban's city alphabet.
PHOTOGRAPHER: Najeebah Al-Ghadban
LOCATION: New York, NY

ROPE "A" Twisted rope is fluid medium for creating any kind of letter, logogram, or pictogram.
PHOTOGRAPHER: Manasrawee Nham Wongpradu
LOCATION: New York, NY

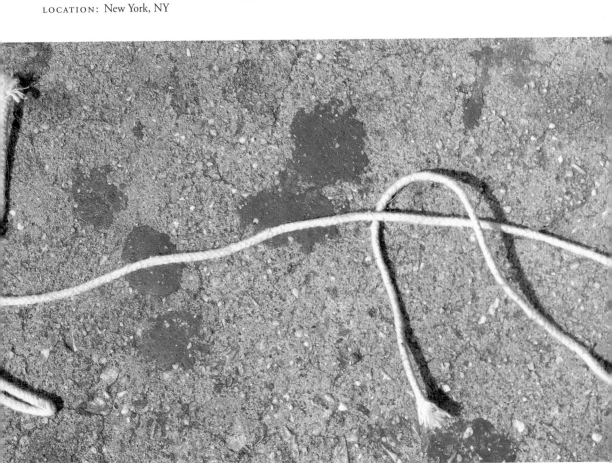

BASKET "Y" An alphabetic shadow cast by a mystery object in a bicycle pannier. PHOTOGRAPHER: Patricia Sánchez Navarro LOCATION: New York, NY

TREE BRANCH "Y" A Brooklyn tree trunk splits into the shape of a "Y."
PHOTOGRAPHER: Kenny Batu LOCATION: Brooklyn, NY

OUTDOORS This project was part of the Cornell University course "Making a Difference by Design," which challenged students to see their surroundings in a different way by analyzing forms and looking for familiar proportions of type. PHOTOGRAPHER: Emelia Day LOCATION: Ithaca, NY

SHADOW "C" "I was on my way to brunch one morning and this trash can turned into a beautiful letter 'C.' Thank goodness for sunny days!" exclaimed Abigail Steinem.
PHOTOGRAPHER: Abigail Steinem LOCATION: Chicago, IL

MODERN-DAY
MONUMENTS

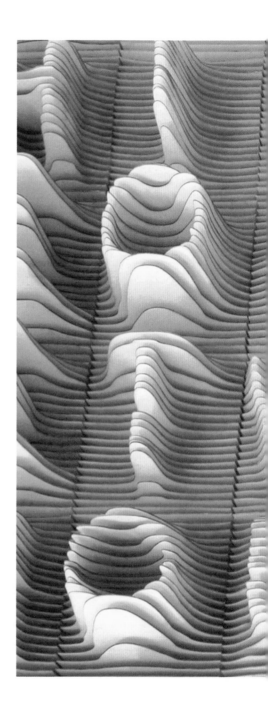

THE ART WORLD HAS FINALLY CAUGHT up with the typographic universe (although some of the very earliest letterforms were arguably made for artistic purposes, inscribed into stones that became the base of sculptures). Today's artists, architects, and public-space designers use stone, marble, metal, steel, and many other materials to build sculptural creations ranging from computer-generated formulations to hand-wrought lattices of letter and word. Some are monumental, others small and pristine. With dimensional lettering, words are seen for what they really mean, and to illustrate what they represent. As letterforms, and especially type, are sculptural by nature, the genre is surprisingly apt, and it has trans-formed a medium so long designed to be virtually invisible.

ALPHABET TOPOGRAPHY "The physical form of language is a record of collective memory," explained Caspar Lam. "In this monotype typeface, the height of the letterforms is determined by how often a letter is used. The typeface maps the rhythmic ebb and flow of English. Each letter sits in a 6×6-inch square, allowing for any combination of letters to run seamlessly both vertically and horizontally." DESIGNERS: Caspar Lam, YuJune Park/Synoptic Office PHOTOGRAPHER: YuJune Park LOCATION: New Haven, CT

SCULPTURAL NET This project dissects the Welsh sentence "*Yn rhyfela gyda geiriau*" (At war with words). The sentence was "reformed using the structure of the net as a base," explained Emma Lloyd. "The basic box form was of interest to me despite its commonality because it is something that will always appeal to our curiosity. For this reason I deemed it appropriate to explore the nature of self, knowledge, and language. All sculptural nets have been inspired by a line from Sylvia Plath's short story *Initiation*: 'So many people are shut up tight inside themselves like boxes, yet they would open up, unfolding quite wonderfully, if only you were interested in them.'"
DESIGNER: Emma Lloyd
LOCATION: Manchester, UK

SPIEGEL This monumental work, constructed in 2010, was part of a major exhibition of sculpture by Jaume Plensa originally shown at the Yorkshire Sculpture Park in 2011. The piece is now in the collection of the Toledo Museum of Art in Ohio. DESIGNER: Jaume Plensa PHOTOGRAPHER: Jonty Wilde LOCATION: Yorkshire, UK

NOT EVERYTHING'S IN A BOOK The University of Ghent's motto is "Dare to think."
This image was used on a promotional poster created for the university by Saatchi &
Saatchi. Its slogan, located in the negative space between books in a library, fits the motto
perfectly. DESIGNERS: Jan Teuling, Ross McCurrach, Arnaud Bailly/Saatchi & Saatchi
RETOUCHING: Beefactory CLIENT: University of Ghent LOCATION: Brussels

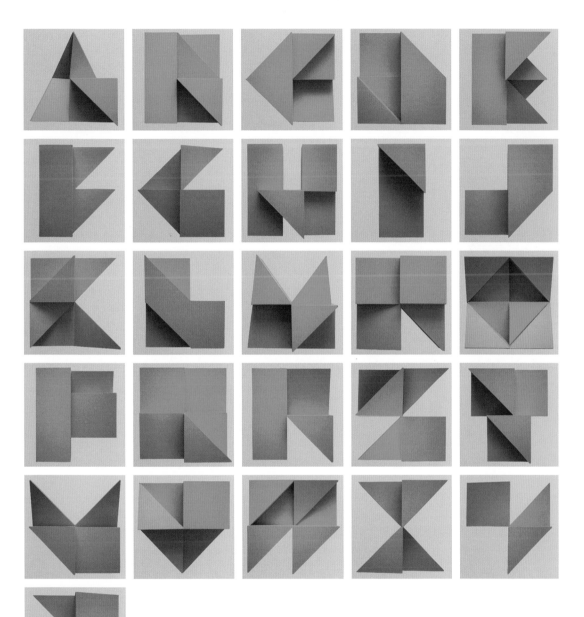

ALPHABET RELIEF Type as "relief." A three-dimensional paper alphabet folded by hand and then photographed. DESIGNER: Tim Fishlock LOCATION: London

BEAUTIFUL BITMAPS Grant Hutchinson combined a love of vintage computers and photography to create a physical representation of a bitmap "H" with several classic-cased Macintoshes from his own collection. "The Macintosh can be considered to be the machine that brought bitmaps and pixels to the masses," he said. This image originally appeared in *Uppercase* magazine's "Beautiful Bitmaps" issue in 2012.
DESIGNER: Grant Hutchinson CLIENT: *Uppercase* LOCATION: Calgary

WORK This large-scale installation was one of many typographic sculptures created both inside and around abandoned spaces in London. The letterforms were constructed out of materials found in situ and the chosen words reflect some aspect of the location. DESIGNERS: Alexander Shields, Jimmy Turrell PHOTOGRAPHER: Alexander Shields LOCATION: London

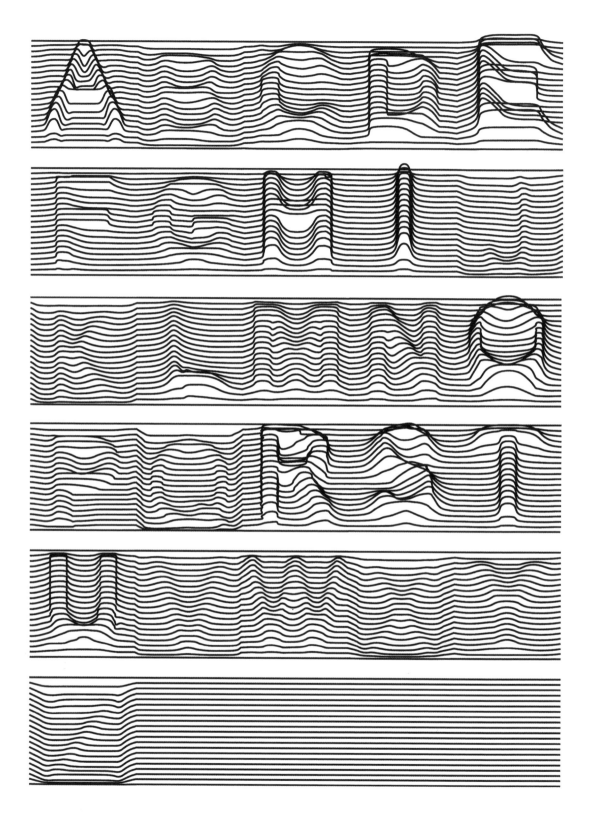

SWELL For this twofold project, the designers at Synoptic Office created "a digital open typeface" as well as an installation of that typeface in which "letterforms reminiscent of the screen are realized by black tape." "The absent digital acquires a physical presence through this complete digital open typeface," they explained. DESIGNERS: Caspar Lam, YuJune Park/ Synoptic Office PHOTOGRAPHER: YuJune Park LOCATION: New Haven, CT

EVOLUTION OF TYPE Made out of MDF, polymer clay, shells, and acrylic, these alphabetic sculptures were inspired by the views of the famous type designer Frederic W. Goudy. In his 1918 book *The Alphabet and Elements of Lettering*, Goudy proposed that letters are a record of the history and development of mankind, and that each separate letter possesses its own essential and organic form. Andreas Scheiger believes that letters are "organisms" and typefaces are "species," all classified according to a system similar to biological taxonomy and sharing anatomical features with human beings. DESIGNER: Andreas Scheiger LOCATION: Vienna

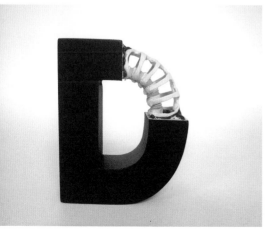

EVOLUTION OF TYPE More typographic sculptures inspired by Frederic W. Goudy's *The Alphabet and Elements of Lettering*. These "surgically opened" letters incorporate models of muscles and bones. DESIGNER: Andreas Scheiger LOCATION: Vienna

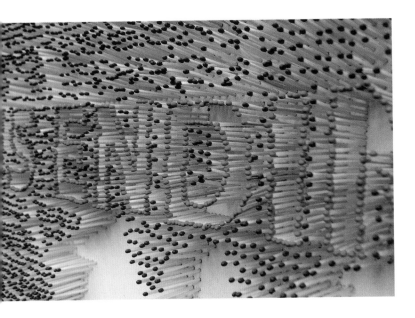

EVERYTHING IS ENDING

An apocalyptic "Happy New Year's" card made up of 5000 matches arranged into the shape of a world map. The collaborative project commemorated the possibility that the new year might never be reached.

DESIGNERS: 3D Neighbours/ Mòn Castel, Javier Jabalera, Júlia Rosich, Pol Trias

ART DIRECTORS: Clara Romaní, Arnau Tàsies

LOCATION: Barcelona

AMPERSAND WIND CHIMES Molly McLeod made these wind chimes for her "Ampersand Project," a collection of sculptural ampersands that engage the senses and the imagination. "I created them using a CNC plasma cutter and carefully arranged different font weights and sizes to produce the finest tones," she said. "What does the Helvetica ampersand sound like? As crisp and harmonious as you might imagine." DESIGNER: Molly McLeod LOCATION: Amherst, MA

EVOLUTION OF TYPE Another design from Andreas Scheiger's ongoing series of sculptures and graphics (see pages 218–22), this fossilized "C" – made from gypsum, plasticine, chicken bones, and watercolors – is a literal take on Frederic W. Goudy's theories on the organic origin of letters. DESIGNER: Andreas Scheiger LOCATION: Vienna

STILL LIFE COMES ALIVE This life-sized typographic installation was made from thousands of pieces of paper folded and glued together to form a sentence that describes and illustrates the concept. The installation transitions from a two-dimensional paper form into a mountainous, organic, three-dimensional structure while still retaining its geometric character. Initial sketches and concepts designed on paper were translated onto a computer before the designers returned to their original medium to construct the final shape. The installation was exhibited at the Concordia University Design program's end-of-year exhibition in 2010. DESIGNERS: Sean Yendrys, Dominic Liu, Stefan Spec, Duc Tran ART DIRECTORS: Kyosuke Nishida, Brian Li, Sean Yendrys LOCATION: Montreal

DECOR TYPE Claudio Scotto used popular fonts to
design letter-shaped home furnishings for a creative
agency. The chair, made from two Din "S"s, evokes
the multi-purpose structure of the letterform, while
the Bodoni "F" lamp lights up the entire room.
DESIGNER: Claudio Scotto LOCATION: Naples

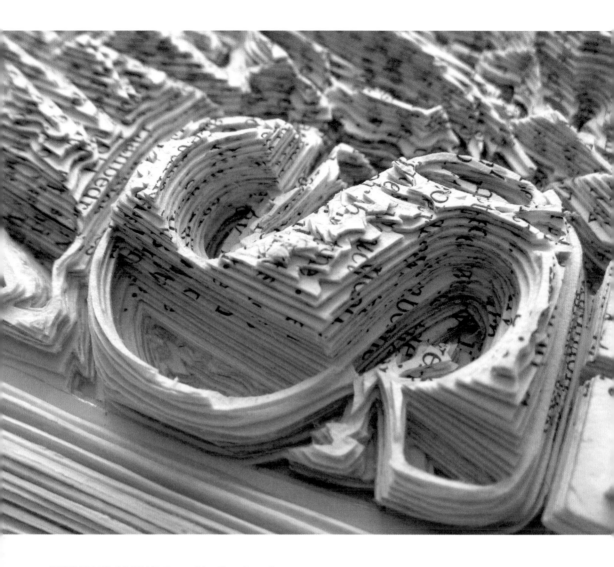

TAMEIDIAU OHONA'I Emma Lloyd's sculptural interpretation
of David Bell's 1957 book *The Artist in Wales*. (See also page 234.)
DESIGNER: Emma Lloyd LOCATION: Manchester, UK

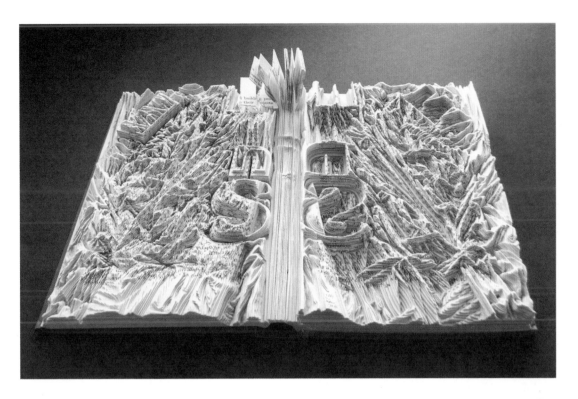

SIT A collaborative installation piece in Hong Kong's Kowloon Park inspired by a poem by local poet Tang Siu Wa "about the freedom of using the public space in your own way." The bench is designed in the shape of the Chinese word "土," which means soil and land. When people ("人") perch on the bench, the action completes the word to "坐," which means sit, "formed by people ('人') sitting on land ('土')." DESIGNERS: Esther Mok, Mia Wu Wing Wa CLIENT: Budding Winter: Art in the Park LOCATION: Hong Kong

TAMEIDIAU OHONA'I A behind-the-scenes photograph documenting the intricate production process behind Emma Lloyd's book sculpture (see page 230). "Here, details are being cut for the middle section of book number four," she explained. "A couple of pages are sculpted at a time with a scalpel – this creates enough dentition for each cut to be visible, yet is gradual enough for the sculpted forms to 'ow.' This process is repeated throughout the entire book." DESIGNER: Emma Lloyd LOCATION: Manchester, UK

PENCIL TYPE Part of a personal study that involved creating typography out of ordinary objects.
DESIGNER: Joe Ski LOCATION: Washington DC

HOPSCOTCH COMPENDIUM A publication cataloging the annual film releases of the leading independent cinema company Hopscotch (now Entertainment One). These sculptural letterforms are from the nine-page cover section of the 2010 compendium. "Each letter was designed using the geometric counter-forms found in the Hopscotch logo, extruded in three dimensions," Mark Gowing explained. "The sculptures transform the ordinary into the extraordinary, illustrating Hopscotch's relationship with artful, tangible storytelling that challenges and inspires."
DESIGNER: Mark Gowing Design
PHOTOGRAPHER: Richard Mortimer
ILLUSTRATORS: Mark Gowing, Vanessa Pitsikas, Dave Foster, Stuart Hall
ART DIRECTOR: Mark Gowing
CLIENT: Hopscotch Films
LOCATION: Sydney

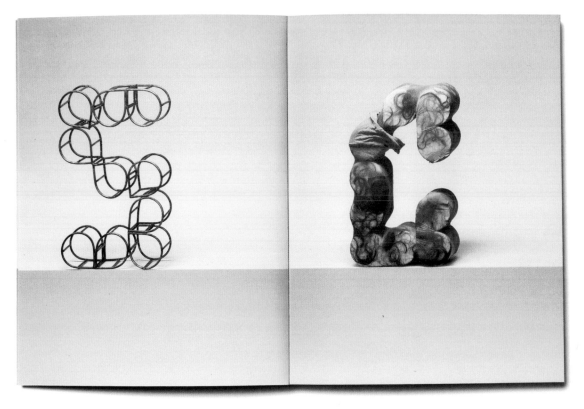

TYPOGRAPHIC SCULPTURES June Corley made this cat and walking man from discarded old signage letters and numbers. The dynamic figures assume comic personas that bring them to life.
DESIGNER: June Corley LOCATION: Loachapoka, AL

FROM SOLIDS TO LIQUIDS

WHEN YOU THINK ABOUT THE ELEMENTS, the Periodic Table may spring to mind. Although elemental types are not as chemically rooted, they are bona fide science experiments involving transient and volatile materials. These are typographic forms that morph and mutate, and must be captured in static frames before they disappear or radically change shape and color. How do you keep hold of something elusive and turn it into something concrete? Graphic designers continue to be challenged by states of flux, and their elemental letters and alphabets are both ghostly and tactile in essence.

EXPERIMENTAL TYPE Billie May used found materials to construct a range of letterforms based on the font Futura. This "U" was created by casting a shadow through a sieve with a card cut-out. DESIGNER: Billie May LOCATION: Brighton, UK

SWEET DUST TYPE Ruslan Khasanov created letters out of photographs of drops of water on a mirrored surface. "After I broke couple of camera lenses I used magnifying glasses," he explained. "I like to play with them to get optical distortions. It is really interesting to see how the simple things that surround us in everyday life, like dust or scratches, have such fabulous properties." DESIGNER: Ruslan Khasanov LOCATION: Ekaterinberg, Russia

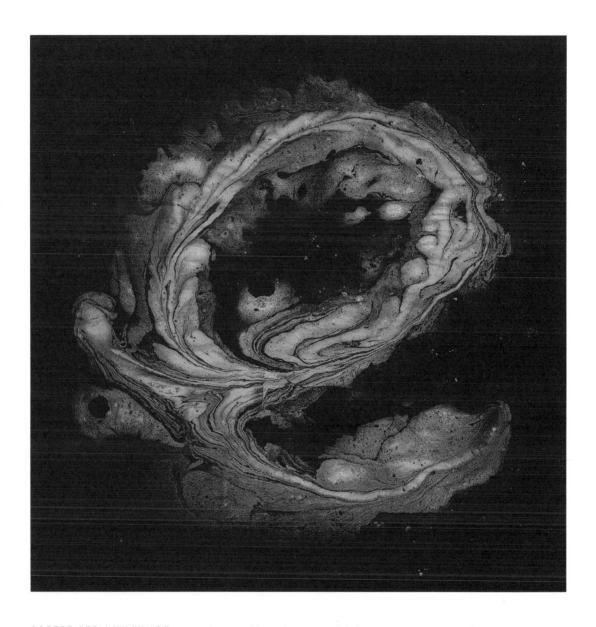

COFFEE "E" / MILKY "R" Letters discovered by Erik Varusio while he was experimenting with an old-fashioned "marble" effect. "The fluid and dynamic quality of this technique emphasizes the randomness and the spontaneous feeling of the resulting images, in which the gesture and the limited control of the medium play their game," he said. "The color helps to give 'substance' and create connection with existing materials." This lower-case "e" reminded Varusio of "the foam that you can see on top of an Italian coffee (but only when it's a good one!)," while the capital "R" recalled "some sort of galaxy, like the Milky Way." DESIGNER: Erik Varusio LOCATION: Vicenza, Italy

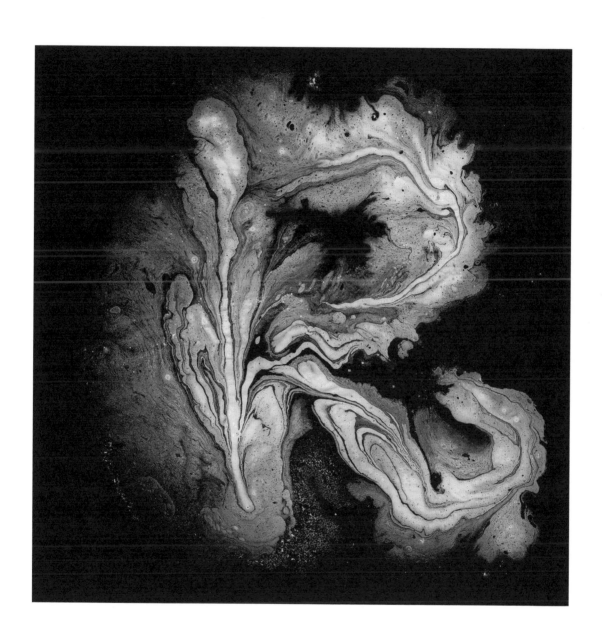

AU REVOIR TYPE Ruslan Khasanov created this liquid typeface while he was designing a wine logo with wet ink on paper to achieve a spreading effect – as though the wine bottle had been lying on a seabed for more than a century and the letters on its label had flowed. While cleaning his paintbrush, he began to draw the letter "D" on the wet sink surface. "The letter came to life," he recalled. "Black, fine lines instantly flowed, overgrown with gray patterns like coral, and then disappeared – like a caterpillar turning into a butterfly and then dying, like a bizarre dance of life, between birth and death. The beauty of the font is in motion, fluidity, and evanescence. My idea was to show how fleeting and fragile the font is in one moment."
DESIGNER: Ruslan Khasanov LOCATION: Ekaterinberg, Russia

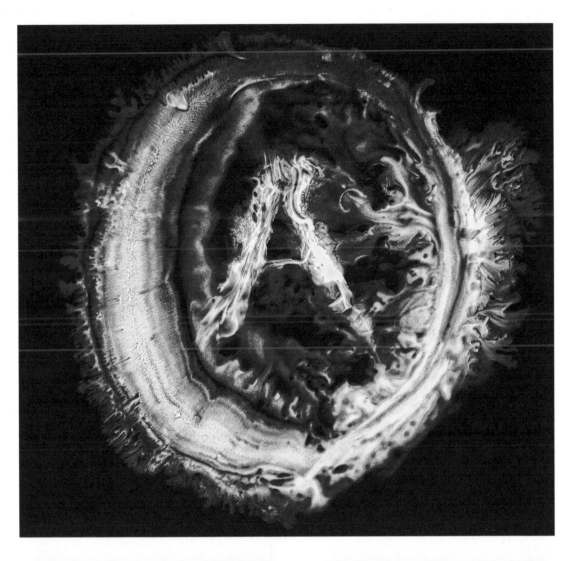

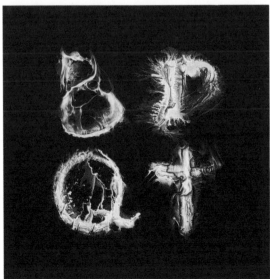

AU REVOIR

LIQUID TYPE Here, letters drawn with ink spread out under a stream of water. Ruslan Khasanov's idea was to show the spreading process in GIF animation. "To achieve the desired effect, I took thousands of photos," he said. "I painted many letters over and over again to get the most interesting plasticity, texture, and dynamic. Whereas the static 'Au Revoir Type' [see previous pages] or 'Micro Type' merely hint at their ephemeral nature, these animated GIFs show the entire birth–death cycle, which I summed up with the phrases 'I've gone away' and 'Odi et amo.'" DESIGNER: Ruslan Khasanov LOCATION: Ekaterinberg, Russia

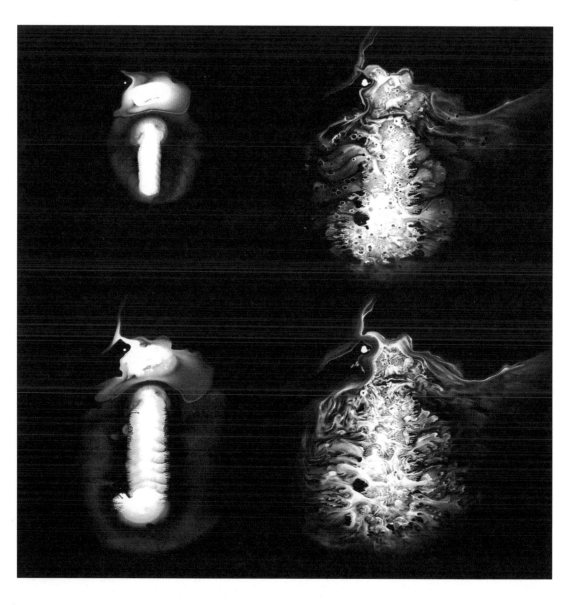

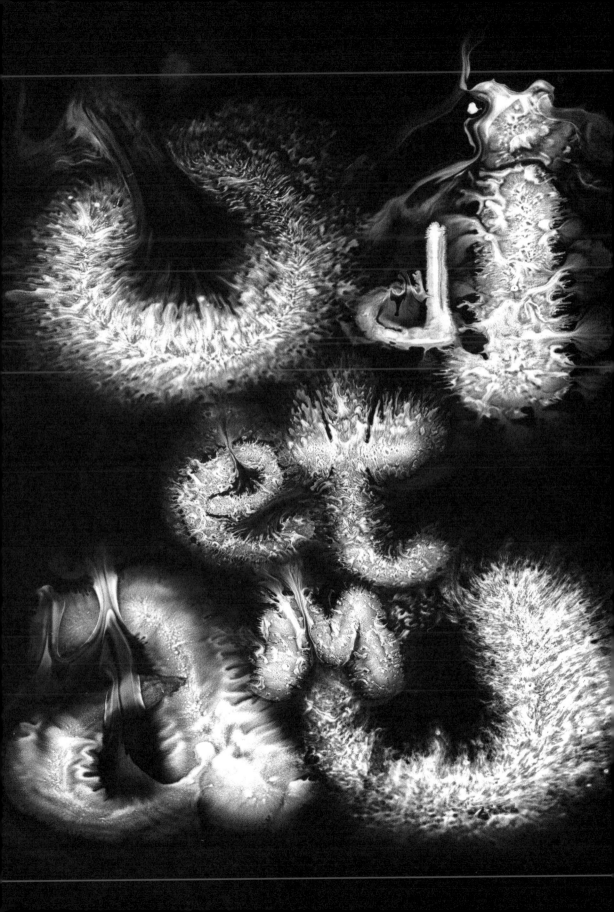

TYPE FLUID An experiment in combining letterforms and liquids. "Fluids and liquids in general look really cool and inspiring," noted Hussain Almossawi, "especially when it's paint dripping or rain pouring down and making beautiful splashes on a surface. That was the inspiration for this project. The concept was to capture the most interesting moments while this happens, while still keeping the letterform noticeable. Once I was satisfied with making my 'a,' I moved on to the other letters." DESIGNER: Hussain Almossawi/Skyrill LOCATION: Bahrain

ICE CUBE "S" While hunting for letterforms in her everyday
surroundings, Julie Wuenschel found magic in an ice tray.
PHOTOGRAPHER: Julie Wuenschel ART DIRECTOR:
Kristin Sommese LOCATION: State College, PA

BLOODY "A" Another letter "found" by Erik Varusio while he was experimenting with a marbleizing technique This blood red, anarchic "A" "revolves like a revolution."
DESIGNER: Erik Varusio LOCATION: Vicenza, Italy

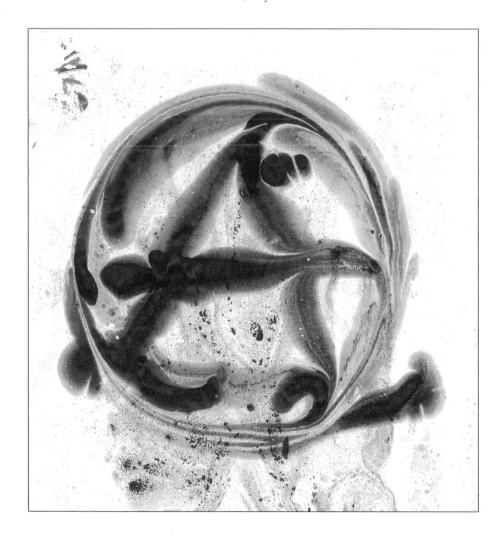

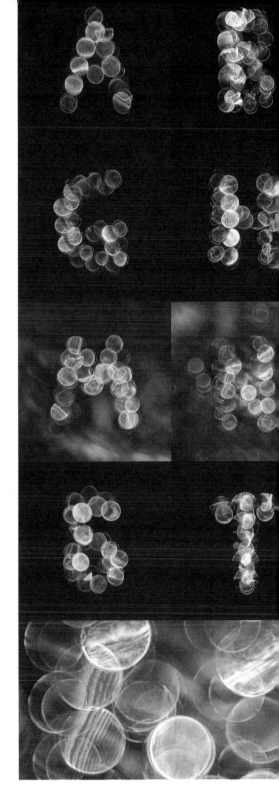

LUMEN TYPE Ruslan Khasanov had the idea for this project while he was out on a night-time walk. "Without my glasses, everything was blurry," he recalled. "I looked at...car headlights – red and yellow circles that floated on the wet road – and I found it beautiful. I did trials after hours in the dark, using a syringe to leave small drops of water on a mirror surface in the shape of tiny letters, then directing a flashlight onto the forms from different angles and distances. A series of magnifying glasses brought out the aberrations." DESIGNER: Ruslan Khasanov LOCATION: Ekaterinberg, Russia

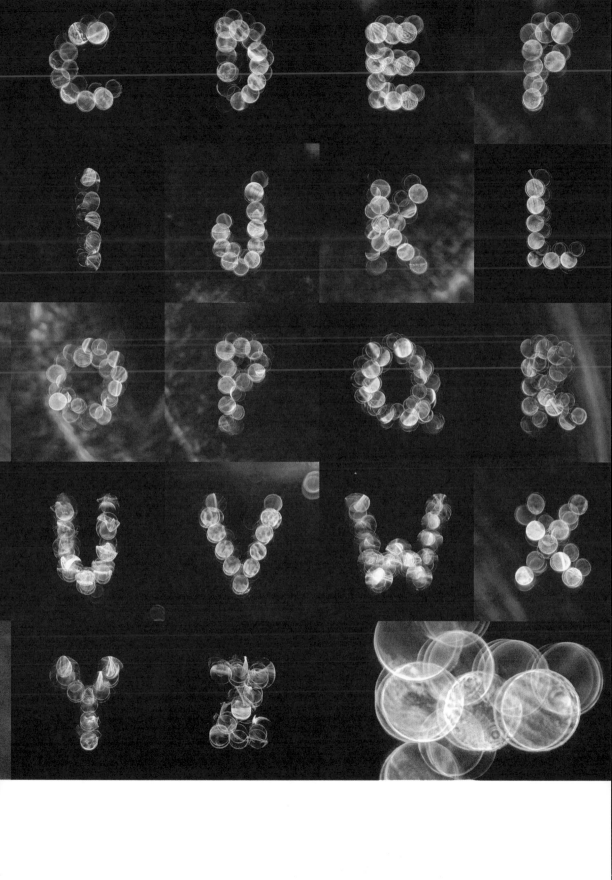

LETTERS IN FLUX

NARCHY IS THE ABSENCE OF GOVERNING CONSTRAINTS. Anarchic type gives the illusion of a similar condition. The paragraph you are reading is typeset within a grid, using consistent leading and word spacing, and with a single type style (excluding the initial cap). The anarchic letterforms and typography in this section are limited by their respective boundaries, but not by any overarching aesthetic or stylistic decree. Instead, they appear out of masses of visual noise and abstract compositions. Some letters emerge, while others are *sub*merged. Some are meaningful, others nonsensical, at least at first glance. The motivation for their display is varied, but all are experimental, testing the limits of legibility and readability, or perhaps exorcising the demons of traditional typographic standards and conventions. Whatever the reasoning behind their creation, you first have to *find* these letters and words before you can make sense of their message.

MAZE TYPE For the 25th project in his "Daydreams & Nightschemes" series (see pages 82, 123, 262, and 267), Jon Newman designed a maze that spells out the words "Happy Thanksgiving" once successfully unscrambled. "Holiday traffic is similar to navigating a maze in that despite how frustrating the process can be, once it's done you feel great and willing to do it all over again," he said. "This project is a visual representation of that frustration and the happy reward once completed." DESIGNER: Jon Newman LOCATION: New York, NY

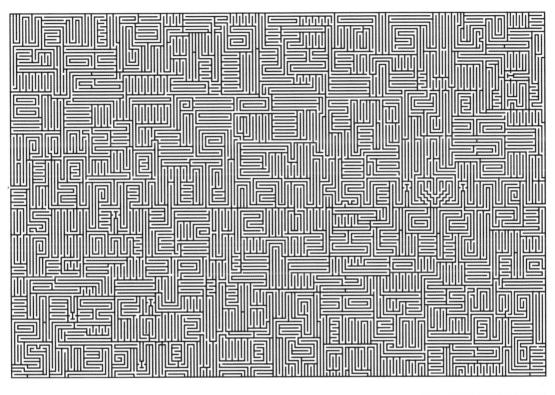

The most impor-
tant things are
the hardest to
say. They are the
things you get

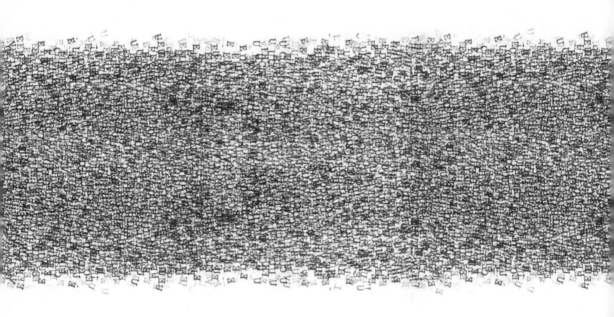

TYPOGRAPHICAL TEXTURE Design students at New York's School of Visual Arts created textu(r)al improvisations within a single page, using photographs of different textures in nature and urban life as their starting-point. Readability, one of the main functions of typography, was yielded to welcome the form's many other communicative abilities – namely the transference of sound, noise, silence, ambiance, and reverberation – which in turn produced these "TEXTiles." By straying from the traditional structure of text as a delivery system for information, the students moved towards the rhythmic textual fabric of light and dark. The results inspired a variety of musicians to "read," "hear," and "see" the new typographical textures as musical notations. DESIGNERS: Christopher D. Wright, Daisy Louise Millard ART DIRECTOR: Olga Mezhibovskya LOCATION: New York, NY

seek convey
m mobile,
to

and
bead g
of stillness

mr.
window
them h
make hu blu
whe h
hat theross
the
who though
throus
hot
of Tok
shadows
The inters
ches
seehie
ng with
so fla
as unown
th
Japanese
and
the the
his head back
find

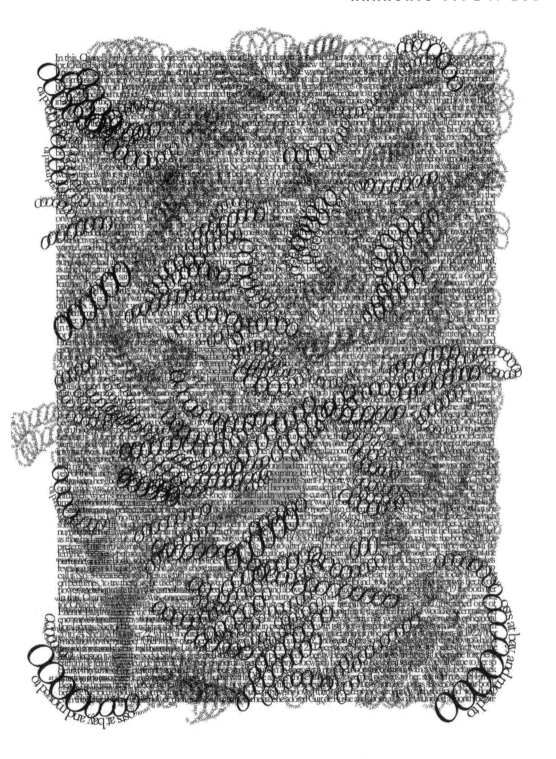

TYPOGRAPHICAL TEXTURE Interdisciplinary experience was at the core of this
university project, which represents a cascade of interpretations on the theme of texture.
Originating in photography translated into typography, these "TEXTiles" eventually
became the raw material for musical improvisations. DESIGNERS: Sirah Yoo, Yuki Murata
ART DIRECTOR: Olga Mezhibovskya LOCATION: New York, NY

REVEALING TYPE The 17th project in Jon Newman's "Daydreams & Nightschemes" series (see pages 82, 123, 256, and 267), this design is based on the concept of visual learning. Each complex graphic hides a quote about vision and art that is difficult to read. Simple, thin bands of color were stretched and weaved to create the illusion of space while using as little information as possible. DESIGNER: Jon Newman LOCATION: New York, NY

HIDDEN DANGER Joe Newton developed this military-style design for "Borgstrand," a font by Swedish typefoundry Fountain. It was created as part of *Kerned Events*, a blog that turned daily news headlines into type specimens. DESIGNER: Joe Newton LOCATION: Brooklyn, NY

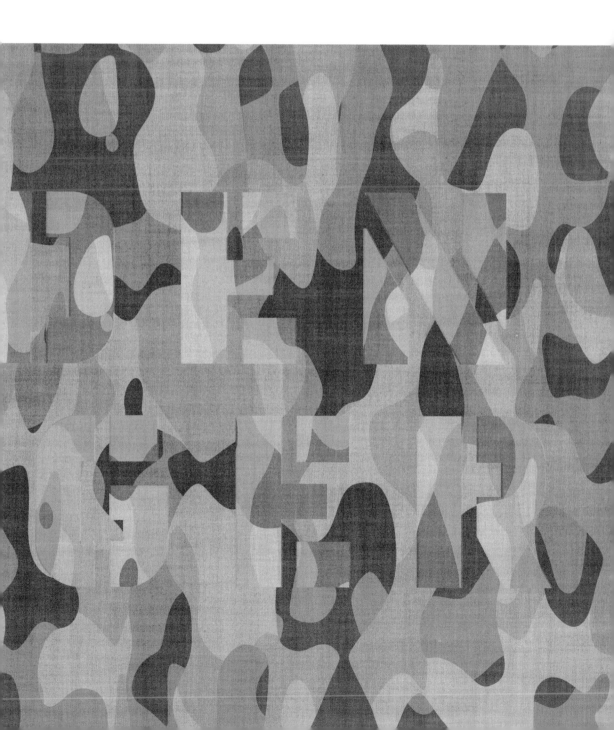

WASTE OF TIME In 2012, AIGA members created nonpartisan posters and videos to inspire the American public to participate in the electoral process and vote in the upcoming general election. This example used the ballot grid as a framework, with text made up of "X"s in the response boxes. The viewer must stare hard at the poster before the message eventually materializes. DESIGNER: Davis Design Partners CLIENT: AIGA "Get Out the Vote" campaign LOCATION: Toledo, OH

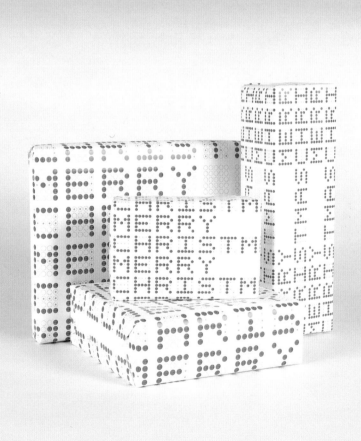

CHOOSE YOUR HOLIDAY CARD This interactive alternative to the typical holiday greetings card was the 30th project in Jon Newman's "Daydreams & Nightschemes" series (see pages 82, 123, 256, and 262). There are "18 groupings of circles containing religious symbols that the recipient fills in, depending on which holiday they celebrate," he explained. The idea was also extended to wrapping paper. DESIGNER: Jon Newman PHOTOGRAPHER: Ka Huen Kwong LOCATION: New York, NY

THIS IS MADE UP Charles Williams created numerous hand-crafted typographic illustrations, some focusing on legibility and others on color. "The idea behind this piece," he said, "was to replicate digital aesthetics using handmade methods."
DESIGNER: Charles Williams LOCATION: London

ALL HUMAN BEINGS ARE BORN FREE In 2008, Tania Mouraud created this installation for the central wall of the entrance hall to the Collège Fernande Flagon. The text is taken from the first article of the 1948 Universal Declaration of Human Rights. "The kids and teachers walk through the hall every day. The piece is made of aluminum and measures 40m². I simply wanted to remind everyone…of this fundamental truth: *Tous les êtres humains naissent libres et égaux en dignité et en droit* (All human beings are born free and equal in dignity and rights)."
DESIGNER: Tania Mouraud CLIENT: Conseil Général 94 LOCATION: Valenton, France

NUMBERS In spring 2013, Berlin's Haus am Waldsee dedicated itself to innovative product design, asking 17 internationally recognized designers to transform the gallery space into a "home." The room allocated to Juergen Mayer H. featured wallpaper, soft furnishings, and pictures covered with translations of data protection patterns – designs developed in the early 20th century to ensure the secure transfer of sensitive information and used to line envelopes, making it impossible to distinguish the text inside. Mayer's patterns can be interpreted as ornamental by-products of the processes of data control. While they relate to 20th-century information transactions, his designs also evoke the contemporary debates around personal privacy in the public domain. DESIGNER: Juergen Mayer H. ART DIRECTORS: Juergen Mayer H., Wilko Hoffmann, Simon Takasaki CLIENT: Bisazza LOCATION: Berlin

NO YES NO DIGITAL ALBUM ART As this five-track EP by the band No Yes No was a digital-only release, Mark Pernice thought he would have some fun with the artwork. "The end result is a unique cover for every person who downloads the free EP," he explained. Each album download "takes an ever-growing database of really wonderful and really horrible album covers (from artists respected, reviled, and also totally unknown), cuts it into tiny little slivers, and bends it to our will." DESIGNER: Mark Pernice DEVELOPMENT: Jon Greacen, Mark Lewis CLIENT: No Yes No LOCATION: Brooklyn, NY

LETTERS THAT BLOOM

HERE HAS LONG BEEN A TRADITION OF CREATING LETTERFORMS
and typefaces out of flowers, shrubs, leaves, and other flora. It dates back to the early 19th
century, if not before, when nature was the most implacable and glorious thing on earth.
Flora played a prominent role in academic design, but when Art Nouveau planted its roots
and wrapped its tendrils around typography in the late 1890s, the floreated madness really
began. Designers and illustrators used all kinds of sinuous and serpentine vines and stalks
until the early 20th century, when the style was cut down by people who believed that
extreme decoration was kitsch. 21st-century designers care less about the philosophical
underpinnings of their inventions and more about creating a visceral sensation.

FLORAL ALPHABET These flowers caught the eye of Anne Lee. "I couldn't resist!" she said. Each individual letter was crafted by hand and photographed in her apartment.
DESIGNER: Anne Lee
LOCATION: Baltimore, MD

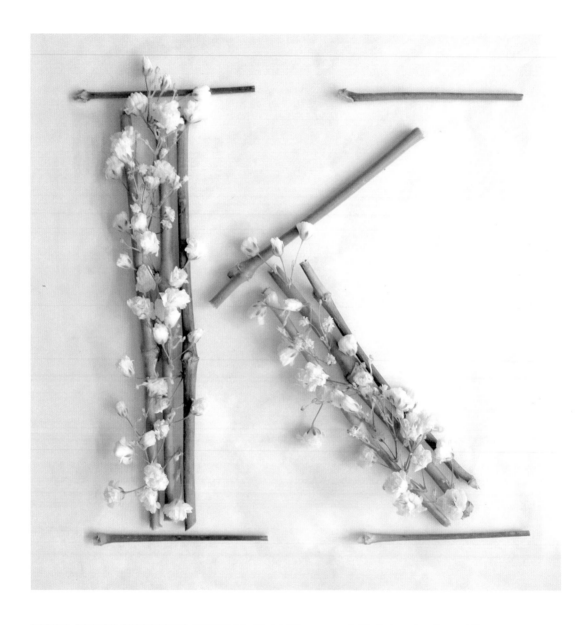

BABY'S BREATH EXPRESSIVE TYPEFACE Keziah Chong created this design using Gypsophila, a flowering plant often called Baby's Breath. "The meaning of Gypsophila is to miss, to adore, and to give," she explained. "Gypsophila often serves a supporting role [as a filler in bouquets], but its existence is significant. This font should have a feeling of freshness, graciousness, and tenderness." DESIGNER: Keziah Chong LOCATION: Gaithersburg, MD

PURPLE FLOWER "*" Another image from a junior-year assignment that instructed students to track down letters, numbers, and symbols in the natural (and unnatural) environment. PHOTOGRAPHER: Julie Wuenschel ART DIRECTOR: Kristin Sommese LOCATION: State College, PA

EYELEAF Marie Bellando-Mitjans was drawing letters with eye shapes such as pupils and lashes when her designs started to look like leaves. She took pictures of three leaves, created a font with the organic shapes, and gave each letter the name of a tree. DESIGNER: Marie Bellando-Mitjans LOCATION: Sèvres, France

FURRY "J" Found and photographed during summer 2013 in Chicago's Lincoln Park. PHOTOGRAPHER: Jane Robert/Francois Robert Photography LOCATION: Chicago, IL © Francois Robert

CLOVER TYPE This "S" made out of three-leaf clovers is an example of Vladimir Končar's "Clover Type," part of his handmade typography project "Diary Type" (see pages 38, 42, 101, 112, 128, and 298). DESIGNER: Vladimir Končar LOCATION: Zagreb

OTKERT TOPIARY A verdant sign for Oktert, one of the best bar/restaurants in Budapest. Sitting on a pedestrian *ucta* (road), the lettering is always being touched and photographed. It's great marketing. PHOTOGRAPHER: Abigail Steinem LOCATION: Budapest

FYNBOS Hand-crafted lettering created for the *i-Jusi Portfolio #2* , which showcased designs inspired by Africa. "While living in Cape Town, I became fascinated with fynbos, which means 'fine-leaved plants' in Dutch," Warwick Kay explained. These plants and flowers are "recognized as one of the six botanical kingdoms and can only be found along the Cape. From a distance they can seem plain and boring, but when you get closer you begin to discover their vibrant colors and intricate beauty. I created this artwork using some fynbos leaves and flowers." DESIGNER: Warwick Kay CLIENT: i-Jusi LOCATION: Cape Town

TOPIARY & TREE TRUNKS Trees
and bushes that turn into letters
without too much manipulation.
PHOTOGRAPHER: Xerxes Irani
LOCATION: Scottsdale, AZ

BLOOMING FONT Flowering letters are an old idea, but thanks to the joy they bring to the senses, they never seem to lose their blush.
DESIGNER: Jessica Tate LOCATION: Portland, OR

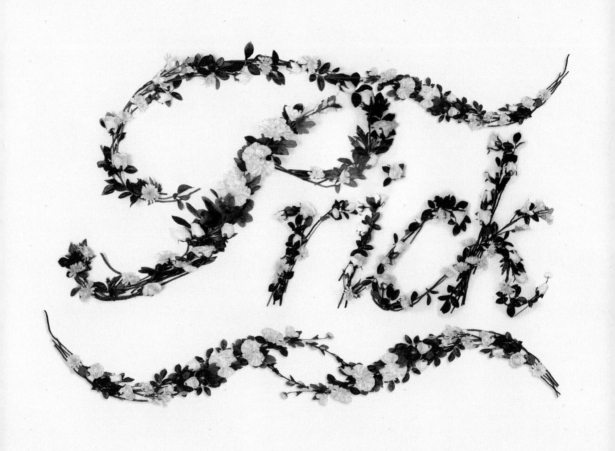

BETTER WITH FLOWERS "Whatever you have to say
will sound better if you say it with flowers," claimed Antonio
Rodrigues Jr. "In this case, it will at least *look* better."
DESIGNER: Antonio Rodrigues Jr. LOCATION: Brasilia

SEED POD "E" A decomposing seed pod spotted in a centenary park. PHOTOGRAPHER: Erica Jung/ PintassilgoPrints LOCATION: Guarapari, Brazil

BOTANICAL ALPHABET These letterforms were made out of jasmine branches. DESIGNER: Jessica Croce LOCATION: Brooklyn, NY

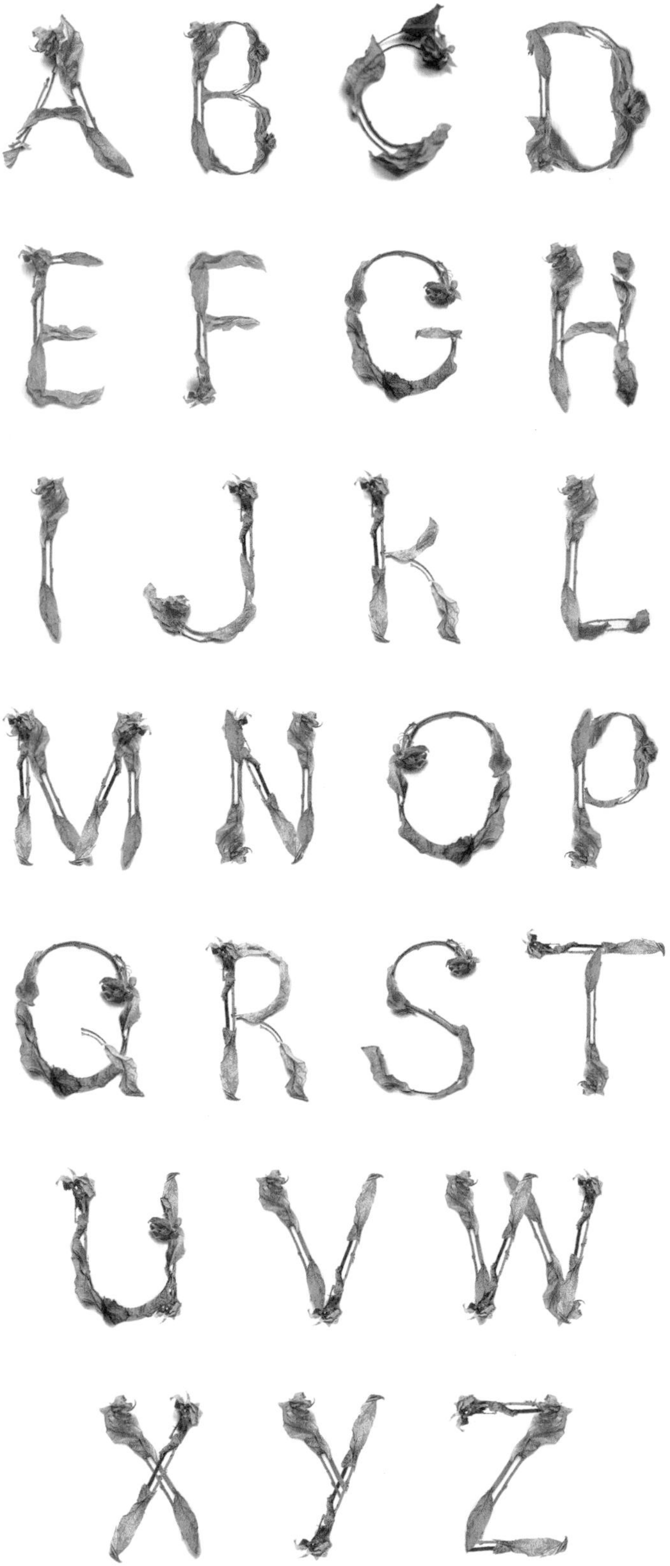
A B C D
E F G H
I J K L
M N O P
Q R S T
U V W
X Y Z

MY GARDEN Petra Bláhová has always been passionate about typography and nature. "You can create typography from anything," she says. "Flowers inspire me with their colors and shapes. I thought of preserving flowers, so I came up with the idea of freezing them." To make her frosted alphabet, Blahova placed flowers and berries in letter-shaped molds and then froze them. "It was very surprising how it worked out. The mixture of the color, texture, and ice created something unique. Every time I look at these letters I think of gardens full of beautiful color." DESIGNER: Petra Bláhová CLIENT: i-Jusi LOCATION: Kendal, UK

CANCER – WHO CARES? Patrick Knowles sought to highlight the work of cancer nurses by creating an ironic message out of real flowers. DESIGNER: Patrick Knowles LOCATION: London

FALL LEAF "V" Another typographic wonder discovered
by Muddyum while exploring the streets of Brooklyn.
PHOTOGRAPHER: Muddyum LOCATION: Brooklyn, NY

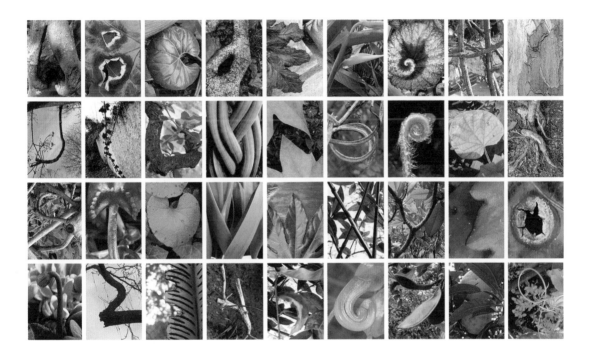

GARDEN DELIGHTS A luscious green alphabet of different plants and flowers. PHOTOGRAPHER: Fabio De Minicis LOCATION: Barcelona

OUT BACKWARD A rejected cover design for Ross Raisin's novel *Out Backward*.
DESIGNER: Robin Bilardello CLIENT: Harper Perennial LOCATION: New York, NY

NATURE'S OWN This mossy "L" and mushroom "M" test
the limits of readability. PHOTOGRAPHER: Tien-Min Liao
LOCATION: New York, NY/Taipei

DECOMPOSING "R" A damp and decaying
still life found and photographed in 2010.
PHOTOGRAPHER: Jane Robert/Francois
Robert Photography LOCATION: California
© Francois Robert

"J" IS FOR JOY More natural letters found
on dog walks through New York's Central
Park. This "J" was paired with an image of the
designer's dog, whose name begins with the
same letter. PHOTOGRAPHER: Susan Klim
LOCATION: New York, NY

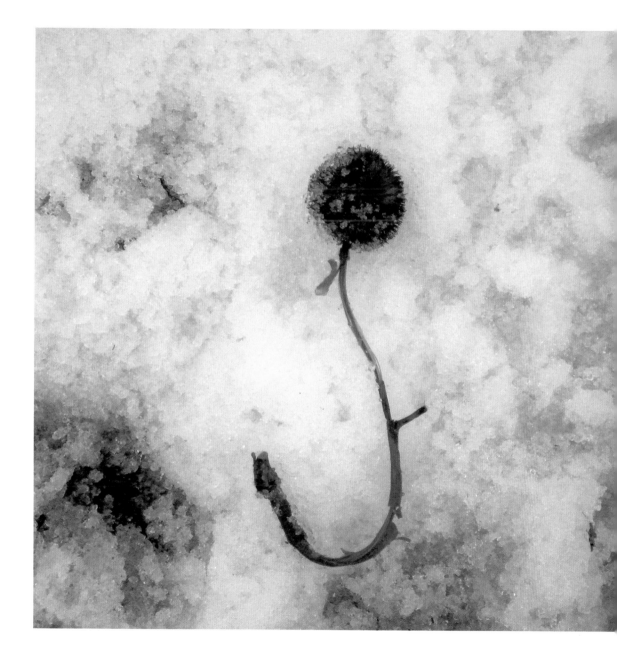

NARCISSUS TYPE Letters made out of daffodils for Vladimir Končar's "Diary Type" project (see pages 38, 42, 101, 112, 128, and 280). DESIGNER: Vladimir Končar LOCATION: Zagreb

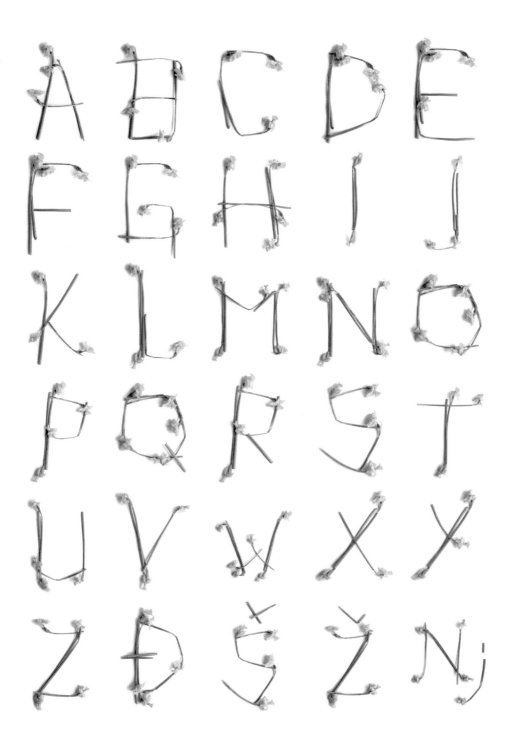

"THIS NATION WILL REMAIN THE LAND OF THE FREE ONLY SO LONG AS IT IS THE HOME OF THE BRAVE."
- ELMER DAVIS

BE BRAVE

IN 2012

BE BRAVE "I wanted to represent American soil," said Virginia Faircloth. "I used a quote from Elmer Davis, a well-known reporter in the 1940s and '50s, and created the word 'VOTE' out of blades of grass that were set in soil." DESIGNER: Virginia Faircloth CLIENT: AIGA "Get Out the Vote" campaign LOCATION: Charlotte, NC

THE ALPHABETIC MENAGERIE

NTHROPOMORPHIC DESIGNS ARE ALMOST AS OLD AS ART itself. Back in Ancient Egypt, intrepid slaves depicted their masters on slivers of bark or stone as animals with human bodies to avoid directly assailing those who might seek retribution. In Medieval times, manuscript illuminators took similar license, turning men into animals and animals into letterforms. The practice extended well into the 19th century, with cartoonists and letterers creating a range of types that appropriated the bodies and characters of different creatures for a variety of reasons. Fearsome wild beasts and domestic pets continue to inspire designers today, proving that the joy of transformation is still in vogue.

"F" FOR FIERCE A children's alphabet made up of retro-modern illustrations that derive from the basic letter shapes (see page 84). ILLUSTRATOR: Paul Thurlby LOCATION: London

for

FIERCE

WE ARE OPEN Verena Hennig created this short film for the opening of her design firm in Nuremberg. "The main actors are more than 500 larvae of the native but rare butterfly species Little Fox, obtained from a breeder in Switzerland," she explained. "The cocooned caterpillars were carefully prepared and arranged on a wall to form the slightly offset sentence 'we are open.' The film shows the words coming to life: the butterflies hatch and flutter away, embarking on their first flight. Thus the film not only effectively announces the 'birth' of the studio, but also subtly translates into moving image the studio's philosophy: the transformation of something gossamer and nondescript into something new and graceful." DESIGNER: Verena Hennig/Meat for the Beast PHOTOGRAPHERS: Verena Hennig, Tobias Binder MOTION: Claus Winter SOUND: Georg Stank LOCATION: Nuremberg

HELVETICAT "Cats and type, together at last." A 12×16-inch design, letterpress printed by hand. DESIGNER: Bethany Lesko LOCATION: Brooklyn, NY

BE GOOD *Wallpaper** commissioned four designers, ranging from intricate illustrators to graphic artists, to create bespoke Christmas cards that were then produced in 250 limited-edition sets. This unique homage to the festive season was made exclusively for the magazine by Finnish duo Anna Ahonen and Katariina Lamberg.
DESIGNER: Ahonen & Lamberg CLIENT: *Wallpaper** LOCATION: Paris

"M" IS FOR MONKEY A linocut alphabet of letters made from animals. "A is for Ape, B is for Butterfly, C is for Crocodile...," etc. ILLUSTRATOR: Mark Long LOCATION: London

"E" IS FOR EEL Each letter in Caitlin Clarkson's alphabet has been rendered as an animal. ILLUSTRATOR: Caitlin Clarkson LOCATION: Los Angeles, CA

"M" BIRD IN STORM Kristin Scheff found objects and animals that resembled letters in her surrounding environment and produced six images for a small book. This photograph was taken in the middle of a hurricane. PHOTOGRAPHER: Kristin Scheff LOCATION: New Paltz, NY

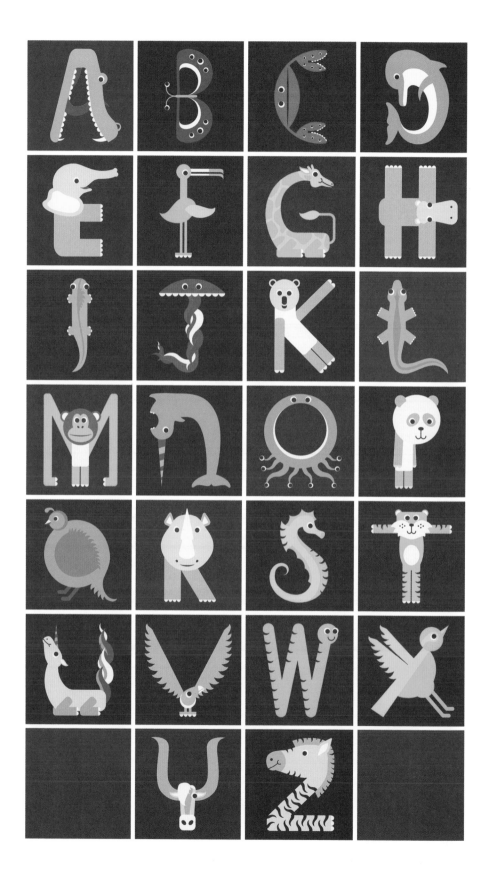

ANIMAL ALPHABET This menagerie of letterforms started out as a contribution to LetterCult's AlphaBattle 2.0, which offered designers the opportunity to express themselves by building alphabets of custom letters over the course of 52 weeks. DESIGNER: Jen Montgomery LOCATION: Los Angeles, CA

CAT-4-CAT Silvia Peressini was asked to produce "a creative representation of any three-letter word." "When I saw my cat sleeping on the sofa, I got this idea!" she said. DESIGNER: Silvia Peressini LOCATION: Rome

THE FADED PAST

T YPE QUITE LITERALLY LEAVES AN impression – many different kinds of impressions, in fact. The types referred to as "ghost" are faded letters no longer in use; the painted remnants of past businesses, products, and services that have been allowed to live on but are scarcely noticed by the passer-by. Despite their loss of function, these relics – even the crassest and most unrefined lettering – possess a dilapidated beauty afforded by the patina of age. Ghost types span decades. While some have been left to fade gracefully, others are marred by graffiti or the elements. And yet all of these elegant, slowly vanishing signs – the Lascaux cave paintings of the commercial and industrial ages – tell us something new about the past.

SWISS MILK, RICHEST IN CREAM This photograph, taken in Bath in 2011, is from *Sign of the Times*, a series of images of vintage signage. The project was "an ode to ghost signs, and the more traditional advertising methods before the arrival of digital billboards and LED screens: graphic design, typography, craftsmanship, and paint." PHOTOGRAPHER: Tom Bland LOCATION: Bath, UK

BULL COURIER Although relatively recent, the rusting, fading, and vandalism heaped on this sign contribute to its iconic beauty. PHOTOGRAPHER: Able Parris LOCATION: Brooklyn, NY

DEWITT'S OTIS These vintage letterforms, photographed for Sam Roberts's research and publishing initiative Ghostsigns, are an example of the heavy Victorian type style in fashion at the turn of the last century. PHOTOGRAPHER: Sam Roberts/ Ghostsigns LOCATION: Melbourne

LIBERTY TIRE They may be primitively rendered, but these letters were not designed by an amateur and were once a real eye-catcher. PHOTOGRAPHER: Maya Drozdz/VisuaLingual LOCATION: Cincinnati, OH

LOW COST HEALTH LIFE INSURANCE
A subtle reminder that three-dimensional
lettering was once attached to this red facade.
PHOTOGRAPHER: Jesse Ragan LOCATION:
Williamsburg, NY

LADIES SUITS, DRESSES, COATS, SKIRTS
Uncovered on an interior wall during renovations, this
typography dates back to the early 1900s. Hand-painted
letters made to last. PHOTOGRAPHER: Jacqueline
Wong/108 ideaspace LOCATION: Toronto

HAND-PAINTED SIGNS OF KRATIE "A celebration of Cambodia's hand-crafted street advertising." PHOTOGRAPHER: Sam Roberts/ Ghostsigns LOCATION: Kratie, Cambodia

THE ROYAL WATERLOO HOSPITAL FOR CHILDREN AND WOMEN
Public lettering in the Victorian style. PHOTOGRAPHER: Sam Roberts/
Ghostsigns LOCATION: London

OIL LAMP GRAFFITI Rough 19th-century scribbles found inside
the Mammoth Cave. PHOTOGRAPHER: Maya Drozdz/VisuaLingual
LOCATION: Mammoth Cave National Park, KY

LE PETIT JOURNAL A faded, hand-painted advertisement for what was once one of France's most prestigious newspapers. PHOTOGRAPHER: Sam Roberts/ Ghostsigns LOCATION: Languedoc, France

THE CASTLE WALL Most of Prague's historical edifices predate the time when advertising began to appear on the sides of buildings. While walking through the grounds of Prague Castle, however, Abigail Steinem came across this sign. "With its black lettering so faded, it felt like stepping back in time." PHOTOGRAPHER: Abigail Steinem LOCATION: Prague

FRESH KILLED POULTRY Simple shop signs were often created by painters without formal art-school training. This particular example has since been torn down. PHOTOGRAPHER: Jesse Southerland LOCATION: Fairmount, Philadelphia, PA

PACEÑA ES CERVEZA A hand-painted beer sign photographed in 2009 during a trip to Bolivia and Peru. PHOTOGRAPHER: Jane Robert/Francois Robert Photography LOCATION: Peru © Francois Robert

MELBOURNE STEAMSHIP During the 19th and early to mid-20th centuries, the sides of most office buildings were painted with the names of the organizations they housed. PHOTOGRAPHER: Sam Roberts/ Ghostsigns LOCATION: Melbourne

1ST CHOICE This ghost lettering is reminiscent
of the 1950s, a golden age. Although the company
is long gone and the times not so golden, the advertising
still stands. PHOTOGRAPHER: Abigail Steinem
LOCATION: Bloomington, IN

UNION PACIFIC The simple log on the side of a long-abandoned railroad car. PHOTOGRAPHER: Michael Stout/VisuaLingual LOCATION: Kelso, CA

SAM CALDWELL & CO. INC. PAINTERS & DECORATORS
A bold, well-lettered, and long-lasting wall sign that befits
the business it describes. PHOTOGRAPHER: Maya Drozdz/
VisuaLingual LOCATION: Cincinnati, OH

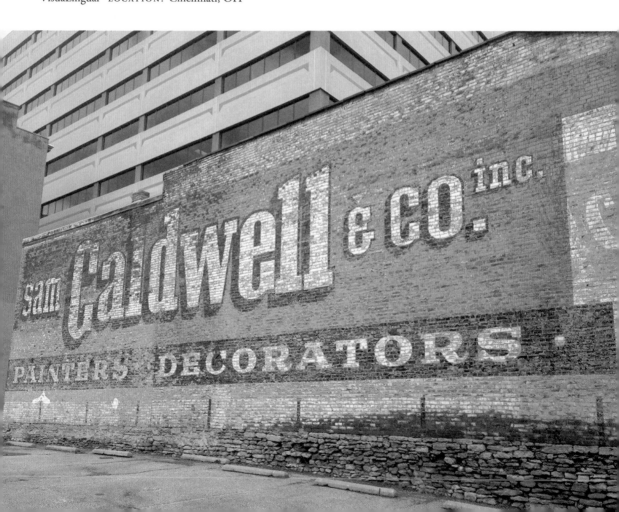

10 CENT CIGAR These cigar advertisements still appear on Google Street View, even though the building they adorn has been knocked down. The signs were found on a mostly vacant street in downtown Elmira, parts of which have never quite recovered from Hurricane Agnes and the flood of 1972.
PHOTOGRAPHER: Paul Stonier LOCATION: Elmira, NY

REFRIGERATORS A vivid relic from
the industrial side of downtown Buffalo.
PHOTOGRAPHER: Grant Hutchinson
LOCATION: Buffalo, NY

DALE BROS. COFFEE A photograph from Marc Shur's *Sign Language* series, a "project capturing vintage signage with its long-forgotten mid-century design and typography." PHOTOGRAPHER: Marc Shur LOCATION: Fresno, CA

ILLEGALLY. ILLEGIBLY. Weathered and distorted
Helvetica on plywood photographed in 2013.
PHOTOGRAPHER: Grant Hutchinson LOCATION: Calgary

STOVES, LAVATORIES, SANITARY FITTINGS
The overlapping of different messages creates a curiously contemporary aesthetic. PHOTOGRAPHER: Tom Bland
LOCATION: London

BOYD PIANOS This lettering, photographed in 2010, is almost pristine in its current state, many years after the time of its creation. PHOTOGRAPHER: Tom Bland LOCATION: London

COCA COLA One of the most internationally recognizable brand logos hand-painted on a Peruvian wall.
PHOTOGRAPHER: Jane Robert/ Francois Robert Photography
LOCATION: Peru
© Francois Robert

TEINTURERIE A fading relic typical of
the directional signage found in France.
PHOTOGRAPHER: Sam Roberts/Ghostsigns
LOCATION: Béziers, France

ANCIENT ORDER OF FORESTERS Gold leaf was traditionally used on official and stately signs.
PHOTOGRAPHER: Tom Bland LOCATION: Edinburgh

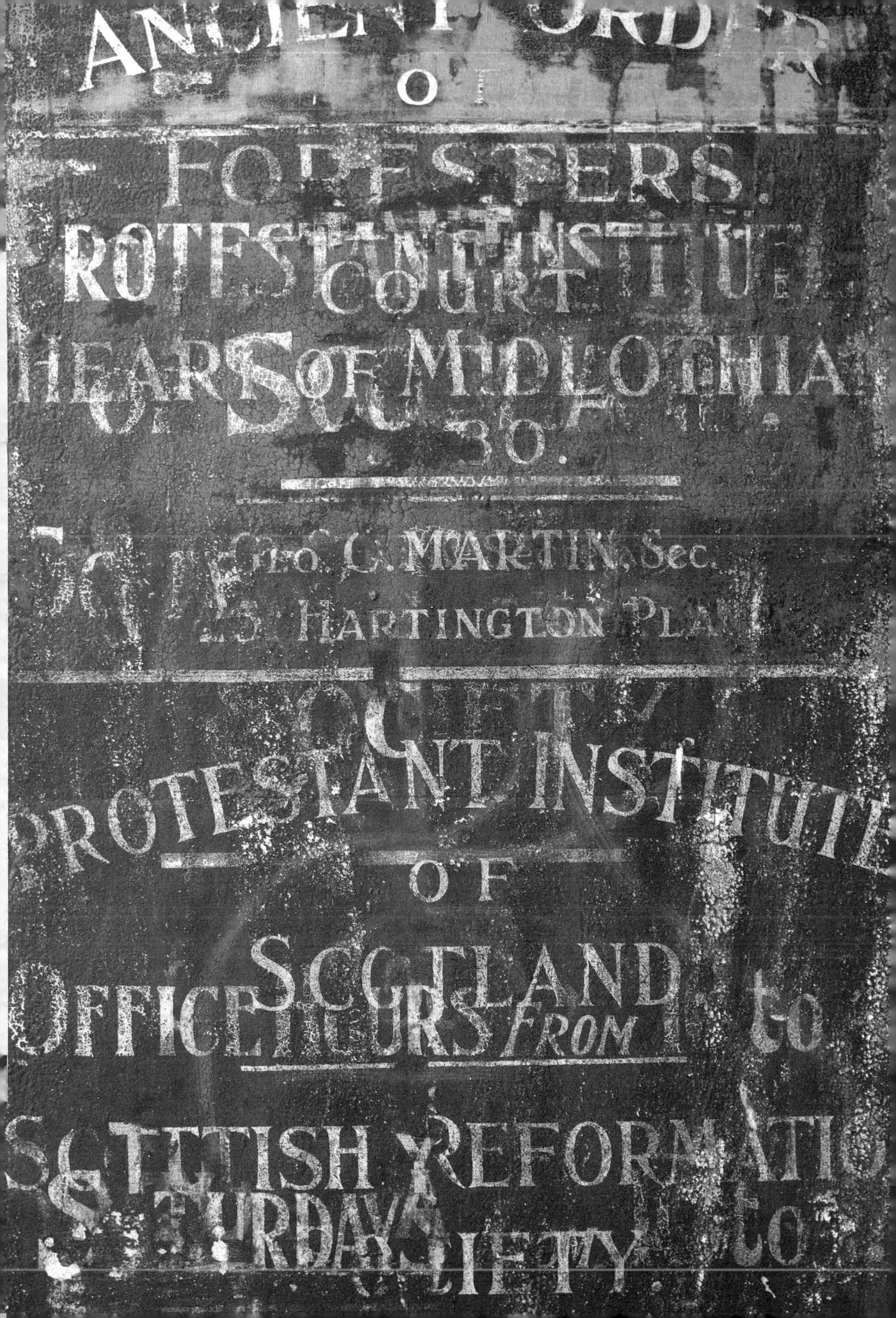

ANCIENT ORDER
OF
FORESTERS.
PROTESTANT INSTITUTE
COURT
HEARTS OF MIDLOTHIAN
30.

GEO. C. MARTIN, Sec.
25. HARTINGTON PLACE

PROTESTANT INSTITUTE
OF
SCOTLAND
OFFICE HOURS FROM   to
SCOTTISH REFORMATION
SATURDAYS
FIFTY   to

DAKOTA MAID FLOUR Painters used these geometric bricks as a grid for their brightly colored design. PHOTOGRAPHER: Jane Robert/Francois Robert Photography LOCATION: Regent, ND © Francois Robert

VOTE Thousands of miles from North Dakota, more bricks are used as a design grid, this time for some sun-blanched white lettering. PHOTOGRAPHER: Jane Robert/ Francois Robert Photography LOCATION: Peru © Francois Robert

FURTHER READING

Baines, Phil and Dixon, Catherine
SIGNS: LETTERING IN THE ENVIRONMENT
(London: Laurence King, 2008)

Bataille, Marion
ABC3D (London: Bloomsbury,
2008)

Blackwell, Lewis
20TH-CENTURY TYPE (New York:
Rizzoli, 1992)

Burke, Christopher
ACTIVE LITERATURE: JAN TSCHICHOLD
AND NEW TYPOGRAPHY (London:
Hyphen, 2007)

Crimlis, Roger and Turner, Alwyn W.
CULT ROCK POSTERS: TEN YEARS OF
CLASSIC POSTERS FROM THE GLAM,
PUNK AND NEW WAVE ERA (New York:
Billboard Books, 2006)

Eason, Ron and Rookledge, Sarah
ROOKLEDGE'S INTERNATIONAL DIRECTORY
OF TYPE DESIGNERS (New York:
Sarabande Press, 1994)

Fili, Louise
ELEGANTISSIMA: THE DESIGN &
TYPOGRAPHY OF LOUISE FILI
(New York: Princeton Architectural
Press, 2012)

Glaser, Milton
MILTON GLASER GRAPHIC DESIGN
(New York: Overlook, 1973)

Glaser, Milton
DRAWING IS THINKING
(New York: Overlook, 2008)

Hayes, Clay
GIG POSTERS: ROCK SHOW ART OF THE
21ST CENTURY (Philadelphia:
Quirk, 2009)

Heller, Steven and Anderson, Gail
NEW VINTAGE TYPE: CLASSIC FONTS
FOR THE DIGITAL AGE (London and
New York: Thames & Hudson, 2009)

Heller, Steven and Fili, Louise
DESIGN CONNOISSEUR: AN ECLECTIC
COLLECTION OF IMAGERY AND TYPE
(New York: Allworth Press, 2000)

Heller, Steven and Fili, Louise
STYLEPEDIA: A GUIDE TO GRAPHIC
DESIGN MANNERISMS, QUIRKS, AND
CONCEITS (San Francisco: Chronicle,
2006)

Heller, Steven and Fili, Louise
SCRIPTS: ELEGANT LETTERING FROM
DESIGN'S GOLDEN AGE (London and
New York: Thames & Hudson, 2012)

Heller, Steven and Fili, Louise
SHADOW TYPE: CLASSIC THREE-
DIMENSIONAL LETTERING (London and
New York: Thames & Hudson, 2013)

Heller, Steven and Ilić, Mirko
HANDWRITTEN: EXPRESSIVE LETTERING
IN THE DIGITAL AGE (London and New
York: Thames & Hudson, 2006)

Heller, Steven and Ilić, Mirko
THE ANATOMY OF DESIGN: UNCOVERING
THE INFLUENCES AND INSPIRATIONS IN
MODERN GRAPHIC DESIGN
(Gloucester, MA: Rockport, 2007)

Heller, Steven and Ilić, Mirko
LETTERING LARGE: ART AND DESIGN
OF MONUMENTAL TYPOGRAPHY
(New York: Monacelli Press, 2013)

Jaspert, W. Pincus; Berry, W. Turner;
and Johnson, A. F.
ENCYCLOPEDIA OF TYPEFACES:
THE STANDARD TYPOGRAPHY
REFERENCE GUIDE (London:
Cassell Illustrated, 2008)

Kelly, Rob Roy
AMERICAN WOOD TYPE: 1828–1900:
NOTES ON THE EVOLUTION OF
DECORATED AND LARGE TYPES
(New York: Da Capo Press, 1977)

Klanten, Robert and Hellige, Hendrick
PLAYFUL TYPE: EPHEMERAL LETTERING
& ILLUSTRATIVE FONTS (Berlin:
Gestalten, 2008)

Lewis, John
PRINTED EPHEMERA: THE CHANGING
USES OF TYPE AND LETTERFORMS
IN ENGLISH AND AMERICAN PRINTING
(Woodbridge, Suffolk: Antique
Collectors' Club, 1990)

Martin, Keith et al.
1000 FONTS: AN ILLUSTRATED GUIDE
TO FINDING THE RIGHT TYPEFACE
(San Francisco: Chronicle, 2009)

Meggs, Philip B.
A HISTORY OF GRAPHIC DESIGN (New
York: John Wiley & Sons: 1998)

Müller, Lars and Malsy, Victor
HELVETICA FOREVER: STORY OF A
TYPEFACE (Baden: Lars Müller, 2009)

Perry, Michael
OVER & OVER: A CATALOG OF HAND-
DRAWN PATTERNS (New York:
Princeton Architectural Press, 2008)

Poynor, Rick
TYPOGRAPHICA (New York:
Princeton Architectural Press, 2001)

Purvis, Alston W.
H. N. WERKMAN (New Haven: Yale
University Press, 2004)

Rothenstein, Julian and Gooding, Mel
ABZ: MORE ALPHABETS AND OTHER SIGNS
(San Francisco: Chronicle, 2003)

Sagmeister, Stefan
THINGS I HAVE LEARNED IN MY LIFE SO
FAR (New York: Abrams, 2008)

Spencer, Herbert (ed.)
THE LIBERATED PAGE (London:
Lund Humphries, 1987)

Spencer, Herbert
PIONEERS OF MODERN TYPOGRAPHY
(London: MIT Press, 2004)

Tholenaar, Jan and De Jong, Cees
TYPE: A VISUAL HISTORY OF TYPEFACES
AND GRAPHIC STYLES, VOL. 1
(Cologne: Taschen, 2009)

VanderLans, Rudy and Licko, Zuzana
EMIGRE: GRAPHIC DESIGN INTO THE
DIGITAL REALM (New York:
Van Nostrand Reinhold, 1993)

Vit, Armin and Gomez-Palacio, Bryony
GRAPHIC DESIGN, REFERENCED:
A VISUAL GUIDE TO THE LANGUAGE,
APPLICATIONS, AND HISTORY OF
GRAPHIC DESIGN (Beverly, MA:
Rockport, 2009)

INDEX OF MATERIALS

The typographic forms in this book are made from an inventive variety of materials. Here is an inventory of the curious things we've found.

CONTRIBUTORS

Ahonen & Lamberg
WWW.AHONENANDLAMBERG.COM

Al-Ghadban, Najeebah
WWW.NAJEEBAH.COM

Alhadad, Mohammed
WWW.BEHANCE.NET/MNALHADAD

Alessandra, Amandine
WWW.AMANDINEALESSANDRA.COM

Alves, Sérgio
WWW.ATELIERDALVES.COM

Anderson, Gail
WWW.GAILYCURL.COM

Appleton, Robert
WWW.ROBERTAPPLETON.COM

Baltimore Love Project
WWW.BALTIMORELOVEPROJECT.COM

Batu, Kenny
WWW.KENNYBATU.COM

Bellando-Mitjans, Marie
WWW.GABIANSPIRIT.COM

Bilardello, Robin
WWW.TIGERETTE.COM

Bláhová, Petra
WWW.PETRAGRAPHICDESIGN.COM

Bland, Tom
WWW.TOMBLANDPHOTOGRAPHY.COM

Brandt, Christian
WWW.CHRISTIANBRANDT.ORG

Bureau Bruneau
WWW.BUREAUBRUNEAU.COM

The Butler Bros
WWW.THEBUTLERBROS.COM

Castel, Mòn
WWW.MONCASTEL.COM

Celiksap, Burcu
WWW.BEHANCE.NET/BURCUCELIKSAP

Chee, Stephy
WWW.BEHANCE.NET/STEPHYCHEE

Chong, Keziah
WWW.KEZKEZIAH.COM

Choo, Ammanda
WWW.AMMANDACHOO.COM

Chua Wenjing
WWW.BEHANCE.NET/WENJINGCHUA

Clarkson, Caitlin
WWW.CAITLINCLARKSON.COM

Corley, June
WWW.JUNECORLEY.COM

The Creative Arms
WWW.THECREATIVEARMS.COM

Croce, Jessica
WWW.JESSICACROCE.COM

Croughwell, Sarah
WWW.SARAHCROUGHWELLDESIGN.
COM

Daley, Megan
WWW.MEGANDALEY.COM

Dashwood, Rhett
WWW.RHETTDASHWOOD.COM

Davis Design Partners
WWW.DAVISDP.COM

Day, Emelia
WWW.BEHANCE.NET/EMIDAY

De Minicis, Fabio
WWW.FABIOBOOK.BLOGSPOT.COM

Engelson, Emily
WWW.EMILYENGELSON.COM

Faircloth, Virginia
WWW.CEDARANDTWIG.COM

Feerer, Ryan
WWW.RYANFEERER.COM

Fili, Louise
WWW.LOUISEFILI.COM

Fishlock, Tim
WWW.TIMFISHLOCK.COM

Foss, Gilad
WWW.GFOSS.TUMBLR.COM

Gajewski, Piotr
WWW.BEHANCE.NET/UPETER

Garcia, Felipe
WWW.FELIPEGARCIA.COM

Goldberg, Carin
WWW.CARINGOLDBERG.COM

Graham Clifford Design
WWW.GRAHAMCLIFFORDDESIGN.COM

Hauser, Graham
WWW.GRAHAMHAUSER.COM

Hennig, Verena
WWW.MEATFORTHEBEAST.COM

Hutchinson, Grant
WWW.FLICKR.COM/SPLORP

Hyde, Troy
WWW.TROYHYDE.CO.UK

Hyndman, Sarah
WWW.SARAHHYNDMAN.COM

Ibrahim, Reham
WWW.REHAMIBRAHIM.COM

Innes, Matt
WWW.MATTINNES.COM

Irani, Xerxes
WWW.FAIRGOODS.COM

Jethi, Nishant
WWW.NISHANT1269.BLOGSPOT.IN

Jung, Erica
WWW.PINTASSILGOPRINTS.COM

Kay, Warwick
WWW.WKAY.CO.ZA

Keenan, Jamie
WWW.KEENANDESIGN.COM

Khasanov, Ruslan
WWW.RUSKHASANOV.COM

Khosla, Ishan
WWW.ISHANKHOSLA.WORDPRESS.COM

Klim, Susan
WWW.SUSANKLIM.COM

Knowles, Patrick
WWW.PATRICKKNOWLESDESIGN.COM

Končar, Vladimir
WWW.KONCAR.INFO

Kurlansky, Mervyn
WWW.KURLANSKY.COM

Lamêra, Sónia
WWW.BEHANCE.NET/SONIALAMERA

Lee, Anne
WWW.ANNELEEDESIGNS.COM

Lee, Raina
WWW.DELICIOUSGRAPHICS.NET

Lesko, Bethany
WWW.ETSY.COM/SHOP/NEATSHOP

Li, Brian
WWW.BRIANLISF.COM

Liao, Tien-Min
WWW.TIENMINLIAO.COM

Lin, Marjorie
WWW.MARJORIELIN.COM

Lira, Rui
WWW.RUILIRA.COM

Lloyd, Emma
WWW.EMMALLOYD.COM

Long, Mark
WWW.MARKLONGILLUSTRATION.CO.UK

McLeod, Molly
WWW.MOLLYMCLEOD.COM

McMorrow, Camille
WWW.CAMILLEMCMORROW.COM

Mark Gowing Design
WWW.MARKGOWING.COM

Mattsson, Kalle
WWW.STUDIOKALLEMATTSSON.
COM

May, Billie
WWW.BEHANCE.NET/BILLIEMAY

Mayer H., Juergen
WWW.JMAYERH.DE

Medina, Pablo A.
WWW.CUBANICA.COM

Mentxaka, Txabar
WWW.BEHANCE.NET/TXABER

Mitsutomo Matsunami Architects
WWW.MMA-DESIGN.COM

Mok, Esther
WWW.SITE.EM-DASH.ME

Montgomery, Jen
WWW.JENMONT.COM

Mouraud, Tania
WWW.TANIAMOURAUD.COM

Muddyum
WWW.MUDDYUM.COM

Newman, Jon
WWW.DAYDREAMSANDNIGHT
SCHEMES.COM

Newton, Joe
WWW.JOSEPHNEWTON.COM

Osborne, Dutch
WWW.DUTCHOSBORNE.COM

Otten, Roeland
WWW.ROELANDOTTEN.COM

Page, Daniel
WWW.BEHANCE.NET/DWPAGE

Pappas, Michelle
WWW.BEHANCE.NET/MICHELLEPAPPAS

Park, Nari
WWW.NARIPARK.ME

Parker, Jonathan
WWW.INSTAGRAM.COM/
CACOMIXL

Parris, Able
WWW.ABLEPARRIS.COM

Pedersen, Eivor
WWW.EIVORPEDERSEN.NO

Pentagram
WWW.PENTAGRAM.COM

Peressini, Silvia
WWW.BEHANCE.NET/IPEAR

Pernice, Mark
WWW.MATICART.COM

Plensa, Jaume
WWW.JAUMEPLENSA.COM

Poisson, Julien
WWW.BEHANCE.NET/POISSON

Prood, Sasha
WWW.SASHAPROOD.COM

Przeganlinska, Aleksandra
WWW.BEHANCE.NET/
OLAPRZEGALINSKA

Ragan, Jesse
WWW.JESSERAGAN.COM

Rienermann, Lisa
WWW.LISARIENERMANN.COM

Robert, Francois
WWW.FRANCOISROBERTPHOTOGRAPHY.
COM

Robert, Jenna
WWW.JENNAROBERTDESIGN.
COM

Roberts, Sam
WWW.GHOSTSIGNS.CO.UK

Rodionenko, Nadya
WWW.NADYARODIONENKO.COM

Rodrigues Jr., Antonio
WWW.ANTONIORODRIGUESJR.COM

Rodriguéz, José Ernesto
WWW.JERDESIGN.INFO

Ryder, Ceol
WWW.CEOLRYDER.COM

Saatchi & Saatchi
WWW.SAATCHI.COM

Saddington Baynes
WWW.SADDINGTONBAYNES.COM

Sánchez Navarro, Patricia
WWW.PATRICIASANCHEZN.COM

Salas, Abril
WWW.BEHANCE.NET/ABRILSALAS

Saporiti, Roberto
WWW.SAPORITI.NET

Scheiger, Andreas
WWW.GLANDIS.COM

Scotto, Claudio
WWW.BEHANCE.NET/CLAUDIOSCOTTO

Sharaf, Mohammad
WWW.SHARAF-INC.COM

Shields, Alexander
WWW.STUCCOPRESS.COM

Shur, Marc
WWW.MARCSHURPHOTOGRAPHY.COM

Ski, Joe
WWW.JOESKI.COM

Skyrill
WWW.SKYRILL.COM

Speck, Pamela
WWW.THEVIOLETFOX.DEVIANTART.
COM

Steinem, Abigail
WWW.ABIGAILSTEINEM.COM

Stonier, Paul
WWW.PAULSTONIER.WORDPRESS.COM

Studio On Fire
WWW.STUDIOONFIRE.COM

Southerland, Jesse
WWW.FLICKR.COM/PHOTOS/
JESSESOUTHERLAND/SETS

Synoptic Office
WWW.SYNOPTICOFFICE.COM

Tabuchi, Eric
WWW.ERICTABUCHI.FR

Tate, Jessica
WWW.JESSICATATE.COM

Temple, Laura C.
WWW.BEHANCE.NET/LAURACTEMPLE

3D Neighbours
WWW.3DNEIGHBOURS.COM

Thurlby, Paul
WWW.PAULTHURLBY.COM

Toormix
WWW.TOORMIX.COM

Tsai, Wanjung
WWW.BEHANCE.NET/WJTSAI

Varusio, Erik
WWW.ERIKVARUSIO.COM

Verbeek, Thijs
WWW.THIJSVERBEEK.NL

VisuaLingual
WWW.VISUALINGUAL.COM

Wang, Irina
WWW.WANDER-CRUSH.COM

Williams, Charles
WWW.MADEUP.ORG

Wong, Jacqueline
WWW.JACQUELINEWONG.CA

Wong, Jim
WWW.GD-MORNING.ORG/JIM

Wongpradu, Manasrawee Nham
WWW.NHAMW.COM

Wuenschel, Julie
WWW.JULIEWUENSCHEL.COM

Yap Ning
WWW.BEHANCE.NET/YAPNING

Zhu, Zipeng
WWW.ZZ-IS.IT

Back page photograph by Able Parris.